SUPERNATURAL
ENGLAND

POLTERGEISTS ◆ GHOSTS ◆ HAUNTINGS

EDITED BY
BETTY PUTTICK

COUNTRYSIDE BOOKS
NEWBURY BERKSHIRE

COUNTRYSIDE BOOKS
3 Catherine Road
Newbury, Berkshire

To view our complete range of books,
please visit us at
www.countrysidebooks.co.uk

ISBN 1 85306 769 5

The cover picture is from
an original painting by Colin Doggett
and cover design is by Nautilus Design (UK) Ltd

Designed by Kingsclere Design & Print
Produced through MRM Associates Ltd., Reading
Typeset by Techniset Typesetters, Newton-le-Willows
Printed by Woolnough Bookbinding Ltd., Irthlingborough

Contents

Foreword

GHOSTS! Belief in ghosts goes back to our earliest history, when our ancestors, like ourselves, sought answers to the eternal mystery of what happens to us after death. Centuries later we are still wondering if reported sightings of spirits and apparitions are proof that there is a life beyond this one. What are ghosts? Our endless fascination with ghost stories gives us tantalising glimpses into the mystery and in making my choices for this anthology it is the sheer variety of phenomena and their intriguing tales that have inspired me.

What do ghosts mean to you? Fear and horror, perhaps? There is the Screaming Skull of Bettiscombe (Dorset), the hideous Croglin Vampire (Cumbria), and Hampton Court's Haunted Gallery where Catherine Howard is still heard sometimes pleading hysterically with cold-hearted Henry VIII for her life. History? Our long and turbulent history has produced ghosts galore, few older than the Bronze Age horseman of Bottlebrush Down (Dorset), and battles ancient and modern have left supernatural traces from the Civil War's battle in the skies at Edgehill to the last war's Bircham Newton airfield.

There's romance too, love that spans the centuries like that of an English clergyman for the beautiful ghost with red hair (Oxfordshire) or the Victorian Lucy Lightfoot and her Crusader (Isle of Wight). In stately homes and council houses, in castles, abbeys, theatres and pubs, everywhere, there are ghostly shadows and so many absorbing stories, some of which you will find in this book. As the poet Longfellow so beautifully put it:

> *The spirit world around this world of sense*
> *Floats like an atmosphere, and everywhere*
> *Wafts through these earthly mists and vapours dense*
> *A vital breath of more ethereal air.*

Happy reading!

Betty Puttick

Acknowledgements

The majority of the stories in this book have been written by Betty Puttick. Some have been written especially for this volume and others appear in books by her.

In addition we are very grateful to the following authors for allowing us to use stories from their books:

Bill Amos for Seeing Things and The Croglin Vampire (*Tales of Old Cumbria*)

David Bell for Dickey's Skull (*Derbyshire Ghosts & Legends*); The Legends of Papillon Hall and The Haunted Council House (*Leicestershire Ghosts & Legends*); and The Ghost in the Ladies' Loo and Driven from His Home (*Ghosts & Legends of Staffordshire & the Black Country*)

Sheila Bird for Parson Dodge to the Rescue! (*Tales of Old Cornwall*)

Judy Chard for Something Out of Hell and The Ghostly Highway (*Devon Tales of Mystery & Murder*)

Jeannie Shorey for The Phantom of Brockley Combe (*Tales of Bristol, Bath & Avon*)

Roger Evans for Sydenham Manor and Things That Go Bump (*Somerset Stories of the Supernatural*)

Ian Fox for Down in the Forest (*Hampshire Tales of Mystery & Murder*)

David Haslam for Nottingham Castle and The Trip to Jerusalem (*Ghosts & Legends of Nottinghamshire*)

Polly Howat for Cambridgeshire Colleges (*Cambridgeshire Ghosts & Legends*) and Scrimshaw's Poltergeist (*Ghosts & Legends of Lincolnshire & the Fen Country*)

John Janaway for The Death of Percy Lambert and Take Me Home
(*Ghosts of Surrey*)

W.H. Johnson for The Bromley Poltergeist and Time Slips (*Kent Stories of the Supernatural*)

Kathleen Lawrence-Smith for The Haunting of Dorothy Blount (*Tales of Old Shropshire*)

Judy Middleton for Golden Ringlets and Mysterious Music (*Ghosts of Sussex*)

Andy Owens for Close Encounters, Heath Farm and Secondhand Spook (*Yorkshire Stories of the Supernatural*)

Marian Pipe for Grafton Regis and Hannington (*Northamptonshire Ghosts & Legends*)

Betty Smith for Gloucestershire Ghosts (*Tales of Old Gloucestershire*) and The Battle in the Skies (*Ghosts of Warwickshire*)

Seán Street for The Durweston Poltergeist (*Tales of Old Dorset*)

Frederick Woods for Godley Green, Tushingham and Stanley (*Cheshire Ghosts & Legends*)

Illustrations

Eighteen of the drawings were commissioned especially for this book from Trevor Yorke (Pages 23, 27, 33, 35, 49, 80, 95, 109, 131, 143, 149, 150, 180, 201, 222, 229, 234 and 252). Thanks go to him and to Bisham Abbey – Sport England (Page 18), Don Osmond (Pages 44, 52 and 74), Nick Wotton (Page 70), Robert Estall (Page 79), *Country Life* Picture Library (Page 153), Eve Dymond-Whyte (Page 163), Courtaulds Films (Page 189), Brooklands Museum Trust (Page 213), Dave Allen and Leicestershire County Council (Page 134), *Nottinghamshire Evening Post* (Page 173).

BEDFORDSHIRE

Black Magic at Clophill

S tanding high on the slopes of Deadmans Hill near Clophill in Bedfordshire is the ruined church of St Mary, a place which became notorious in the 1960s and 1970s after a macabre series of events suggested that in this quiet English village the ancient evil rituals of black magic and necromancy were very much alive and still being practised.

One climbs a long, narrow track overhung with trees to reach the ruined church, the gravestones now ranged round the edges of the grassed-over burial ground like a row of watchful grey figures. The ancient church still retains its tower, the nave just a roofless shell with a few strange hieroglyphics scrawled on the inner walls. The site has been tidied up since the days when the churchyard was an overgrown wilderness, its gravestones leaning crazily, but many people still sense an oppressively evil atmosphere in this place where ghoulish vandalism once wreaked havoc.

It was in March 1963 that seven altar tombs in the churchyard of St Mary's were found to have been damaged. Unknown vandals had apparently attempted to dislodge the heavy stone slabs, but found the entrances to six of the tombs sealed by brickwork. Finally they managed to gain entry into the grave of Jenny Humberstone, the young wife of an apothecary, who died in 1770 at the age of 22. The coffin had been broken open and the skeleton removed.

Jenny's bones were discovered in the church arranged in a circle, with a cockerel's feathers scattered nearby. It is said that a child was seen playing with the skull, which had been found impaled on an iron spike.

Was this some kind of grisly hoax? It seemed likely that there was a more sinister explanation such as necromancy, an ancient magical ritual aimed at communicating with the spirits of the dead, and in which a corpse played an essential part. Inevitably the weird happenings at Clophill attracted the attention of the press and television reporters, who were all agog to discover every macabre detail, and to the distress of the parish priest, curious sightseers invaded the village, causing even more damage and desecration to the church and graveyard.

Eric Maple, the writer on ghosts and witchcraft, visited the site on behalf of the Associated Rediffusion programme *This Week* in March 1963. He said afterwards: 'There was an atmosphere I can only describe as absolutely evil and I never wanted to go there again.' A ladder was put into the grave which had been desecrated, and he was expected to make his commentary from the depths 'among the bones'. He was so overcome by the sensations induced by his macabre surroundings that he fainted, to the disgust of the cameramen who were chiefly concerned about the waste of film! 'All the time we were there I had the horrible feeling that something or somebody was watching over us,' Maple said afterwards.

Meanwhile, the vicar had removed poor Jenny's bones to a place of safety; but the vandals apparently returned soon afterwards and, finding the skeleton gone, angrily broke up what was left of her coffin and threw the pieces about the church and churchyard. Later on, Jenny's remains were finally reburied in her former grave by the church porch, with 8 tons of earth on top to keep her safe from further desecration.

Six years after these events another tomb was damaged in what appeared to be a similar attempt to remove the body. The vicar bravely kept vigil for a couple of nights, but on the third night when all seemed to be quiet he went home, only to find next day that two more graves had been damaged. And again in 1975 human remains were removed from a tomb and scattered about by unknown vandals. A local newspaper reporter who visited the ruined church at the time discovered a human skull lying on the ground near the damaged tomb, and also a small statuette of the Virgin Mary with the head broken off.

With such a grim history, it is not unreasonable to imagine that Clophill's ruined church and graveyard might well be the haunt of disturbed spirits. One dull, wet November day Mr Tony Broughall and his wife visited the ruins and took photographs. They had the place to themselves, so when the pictures were developed they were surprised to find that one included a figure in white by the south window of the church facing down the nave, and they were unable to find any possible explanation to account for it. On subsequent visits to the site Mr Broughall took a number of photographs from the same position in an attempt to duplicate the original picture, but the mysterious ghostly figure never appeared on any of them.

'It was all the more puzzling because the floor of the church is at least 6 feet below the bottom of the window,' said Mr Broughall. 'Which means that the figure was apparently some 6 feet above ground level.'

It occurred to him later that one possibility could be that the figure was an apparition of a clergyman standing where the pulpit would have been.

Some time later he met a Dunstable schoolmaster who had been allowed by the church authorities to take a small group of senior pupils to undertake a 'dig' in the church interior. They had found a cross bound with reeds buried where the altar formerly stood, and a doll daubed with strange symbols which was buried at the tower end. In the nave they excavated a tomb containing two skeletons, and they also found a coffin nameplate with the name Sophia Mendham, giving the date of death as 1893.

Mr Broughhall discovered that some of the older local inhabitants believed that the ruins were haunted by 'Sophie's ghost'. So had his photograph managed to capture her wraith, or was it some other long-gone resident of Clophill's much disturbed graveyard which appeared so mysteriously on his print?

In the *Bedfordshire Times* of 6th August 1971, another uncanny encounter was reported.

Just after Christmas 1969 a Haynes newsagent, Mr Lawrence Steinmetz, was delivering newspapers to Northfields Farm on the Haynes Church End to Clophill road when he saw a small light approaching. Thinking it was a cyclist, he dipped his headlights and slowed down; he could then see that it was a man on horseback, carrying a lantern.

Mr Steinmetz stopped his car and turned off the lights, and as the rider drew nearer he saw that it was a hooded man 'like a monk'. To his alarm, horse and rider came straight on towards him and rode right through the car.

'My wife and I were terrified,' he said, 'we daren't look behind and I just put my foot down and rushed off. It was a horrible experience.

'We did not mention this to anybody at the time, but about a year later a lady asked us if we had ever met, on our early morning deliveries, a man in a cloak on horseback on the Clophill road. She said she had lived in the house on the hill just before the drive to Northfields Farm, but the family had been so upset by the ghost that they had moved.

'When I told the story to a farmer in Haynes, he produced from his barn a horn lantern exactly like the one our ghost carried, which he said was well over 200 years old.'

Mr Steinmetz thought the ghost was probably on his way to Chicksands Priory. 'The farm drive runs almost parallel to where I believe there used to be a track to the old Priory,' he said.

❖

The Little Blue Man at Studham

S tudham is a pleasant little village beside a common, at the end of which a footpath leads to a small overgrown area surrounded by bushes and trees, near to the school. They call it the Dell, and when I have been there it seemed to me that this rather claustrophobic little valley full of bracken and gorse bushes has a still, slightly strange atmosphere, as if anything could happen. And one day, apparently, it did!

The unusual events of 28th January 1967 began dramatically enough with a single flash of lightning, and the rumble of thunder. It had been raining, and when it stopped seven boys were in the Dell on their way back to school after lunch at about 1.45 pm. One boy, Alex Butler, aged 10, was a little ahead of the others, and he was standing on top of the surrounding bank overlooking the centre of the Dell when to his surprise he noticed 'a little blue man with a tall hat and a beard' standing quite still at the foot of the opposite bank.

For a moment or two Alex stared at this unfamiliar stranger, and then he shouted to summon his friends who came running; like Alex, they too stared in amazement at the unusual sight. Then with one accord they ran down the bank towards the odd little character who stood immobile not more than 20 yards away. At this point a strange whirling cloud of yellowish-blue mist was discharged towards the boys, and the little man disappeared.

Undaunted, the boys began to search for him, running through the Dell and up the bank, and suddenly there he was again, further along the bank. As before, he was about 20 yards away from them, standing quite still, and as the boys came closer, he disappeared again.

When the boys reached the place where the little man had been there was no trace of him, but as their eyes scanned the Dell in search of the elusive little creature, they spotted him down at the bottom of the Dell, not far from where Alex had first seen him. And then something else rather curious and inexplicable happened.

As they stared down at the little figure standing as immobile as before, they heard something they afterwards described as 'voices not like a human'. The sound was more like a continuous, deep, 'foreign-sounding' babble of noise which stopped the boys in their tracks. Were there perhaps more little men hidden somewhere in the bushes who were communicating with the first one? The curious murmur of sound seemed to be coming from somewhere closer to them than the little man, and cautiously the boys circled the Dell, looking down to where he stood, still in the same place, and still apparently rigid and unmoving.

As they hesitated, uncertain what to do next, they heard the sound of their teacher's whistle from Studham Primary School, and the boys hurried off, brimming over with excitement, to tell Miss Newcomb about their extraordinary experience.

It is to Miss Newcomb's credit that after listening to what seven of her pupils had got to say, far from dismissing their unusual story as nonsense, she made them all write down in their own words what had happened, making sure that there was no collusion. After tidy copies had been made, they were pasted in a special book entitled 'The Little Blue Man on Studham Common'.

So what did that group of 10 and 11 year old friends see that winter afternoon? A little man in blue with a black belt and a tall hat and beard sounds uncommonly like Noddy's friend, Big Ears. Although the Dell is not far from a row of houses and the school, it is quite a wild area. Could it possibly be that with the clear eyes of childhood the boys had seen some kind of nature spirit, or even a brownie in the Enid Blyton mould?

A reader of *Flying Saucer Review* saw a short reference to 'a little blue man at Studham' in the *Dunstable Gazette* of 3rd March 1967. It contained the remarkable information that the boys had seen a blue man, with blue clothes and blue hair. One child described him as 'blue all over his body, with big ears [!], a funny nose and shageu [shaggy] blue hair. I and my friends were startled, he was horrid.' Despite the big ears, one begins to realise that this strange entity was unlikely to be the kind to feature in any Enid Blyton story.

The magazine was contacted and three people from *Flying Saucer Review* visited Studham to meet the boys and their teacher. After seeing the places where the little blue man had appeared, they were able to go into more detail with the children.

During their four brief encounters with the little blue man, the boys' sharp eyes had missed little. They agreed that he was about 3 feet high, with a tall hat or helmet with a rounded top like a brimless bowler which added another 2 feet to his height. His blue colour was more of a dim greyish-blue glow, and he had two round eyes, a kind of flat triangle in place of a nose, and he was wearing a one-piece garment with a broad black belt which had a black box on the front about 6 inches square.

The little man's arms were short and remained straight down at his sides, but his legs and feet were misty and hard to discern. The boys described him as having a beard, and when questioned they said it divided below the chin and ran down both sides of his chest. The idea that this could have been some kind of breathing apparatus was suggested and the boys agreed that this was possible, but they had not been able to see it clearly enough to know, and this thought had not occurred to them at the time.

The boys had been remarkably observant and made no attempt to embroider the facts as they saw them; their teacher, and everyone else who heard their story, had no doubt that they were speaking the truth, and that this unusual incident really happened.

As far as I know, nothing else emerged then or has done since to explain this intriguing encounter. Could the blue man have been an alien? Or a robot? Was the black box on his belt used to send out the cloud of mist to hide his tracks so that he could evade his pursuers by hiding in the bushes? Or did he really disappear when he played his game of hide and seek with the boys? And where were the strange voices coming from? Possibly the black box was a receiver. Was there some kind of UFO parked conveniently nearby? Certainly no one reported seeing anything of the kind.

I'm afraid the little blue man on Studham Common must remain a mystery. But one thing I am sure of: it wasn't Big Ears!

BERKSHIRE

The Ghost With a
Guilty Conscience

I stared at Dame Elizabeth Hoby, and she, imperious in her Elizabethan widow's weeds, stared icily back.

After nearly four hundred years the full length portrait seemed faded in the dim light of the panelled hall at Bisham Abbey, but two things stood out. Against her long black gown her hands, with their sharp, tapering fingers, looked white, almost bloodless, and in that haughty face most of all I noticed her eyes, dark, hard and bright as a predatory bird's.

In life Dame Hoby must have been an uncomfortable person to meet. And now? Standing there beneath her portrait I remembered uneasily that her restless spirit has roamed her old home for centuries. Involuntarily I shivered, and thought I shouldn't like to meet you, Dame Hoby, either dead or alive.

The old stone Abbey with its pointed gables stands by the Thames in Berkshire. Steeped in history it has known Elizabeth I, Anne of Cleves, Oliver Cromwell and many others. Today it is a National Sports Centre where top flight sportsmen and women train, and there are also courses in all kinds of sport and recreation.

Ancient flags, cobweb-fine with age, hang from the minstrels' gallery in the hall which is now the students' dining room. Outside the magnificent beech woods facing the Abbey were hazy with mist on the day I was there. Local gossip has always warned against wandering down by the river in misty autumn weather, or 'wicked Lady Hoby' might lead you to certain death in the water.

Two boys, on their way back from a fishing trip one evening at dusk, were badly frightened when they saw a boat by the river bank. In it sat an old woman, huddled in her black hooded cloak. It might have been Dame Hoby, but they didn't wait to find out!

Miss Margaret Dickinson, whose family used to own the Abbey, told me that Dame Hoby's ghost was accepted by the family, although 'I have never seen anything myself,' she added.

However, Miss Dickinson knows all about Dame Hoby's personal appearances. For example, one young man staying at the Abbey when the house was crowded with guests for the Henley Regatta was put up for the night in the library. Like many youths his curly hair was his pet vanity. No one knows how the ghost could have been aware of this, but during the night he woke to see the spectre of Dame Hoby, her long fingers reaching out towards him! 'Young man,' she said, 'if I but touch thee, thou wilt be bald'. When the light of day dawned, and he found his hair was still intact, the visitor left hurriedly and became a clergyman!

There was another case of a girl staying at the Abbey who went to bed early one night. For a while she sat up reading in her four-poster bed, her little dog beside her. Suddenly the dog, its hackles rising, leapt off the bed and shot out of the room, apparently terrified by something.

The astonished girl first saw her watch being lifted from her bedside and thrown across the room by an invisible hand. Next, a pile of sheet music was overturned, and a toilet set knocked over. Then the curtains of the bed were wrenched off violently and the frightened girl saw a woman wearing what appeared to be an old-fashioned nightgown, standing by the end of the bed.

In a state of shock she ran out of the room and downstairs to the other guests in the hall. Later when she was shown Lady Hoby's portrait, she recognised her hostile visitor at once!

One of the odd aspects of Lady Hoby's haunting is that she is seen in the 'negative', that is, her huge floating white headdress, ruff and frilled sleeves appear black, and her black gown is white. She has been

Dame Elizabeth Hoby of Bisham Abbey

observed drifting through the Abbey, a bowl before her, and like a grief-stricken Lady Macbeth, she repeatedly washes her hands, trying to remove the traces of her guilt – for she is reputed to have murdered one of her sons.

Clever and intellectual like her diplomat husband, Elizabeth Hoby was determined that her boys should do her credit. The eldest, Edward, eventually became an important man at Court, but Thomas, who was born after his father's early death, was to his mother's disgust, undersized and something of a laughing stock. However, tradition says there was another son, William, who was also a disappointment to his mother. In those days very high standards were expected of quite young children, and Dame Hoby had no patience with William's blots and smudges as he struggled miserably with his writing. Enraged at his stupidity one day, she hit him so violently about the head that he died.

Another version says that she tied him to a chair and left him alone in a tower room as a punishment. Then, forgetting to tell the servants he was there, she had gone off to Windsor with her friend Queen Elizabeth, and when she came back, the child was dead. Yet another story says that the writing lesson took place in a summerhouse by the river, and villagers actually witnessed her savage attack on the boy, who collapsed dying on the grass.

Dame Hoby married twice and had several children, some dying in infancy, but, oddly enough, no record of William's short life exists. It seems, though, that the persistent stories must have had some foundation. But the family was a powerful one. Was it possible that Dame Hoby's dreadful secret was hushed up to the extent of destroying evidence that William was ever born?

One might dismiss the whole thing as a legend, except for some evidence that came to light in 1840. Part of the Abbey's dining room floor was taken up during alterations and among the rubble stuffed underneath some old papers were found. Several of these turned out to be Elizabethan copy books, and Mrs Vansittart who was at the Abbey at the time found out that they had belonged to the Hoby family. 'I wanted to take two or three away with me, but my sister-in-law wished to keep them till Admiral Henry Vansittart, a relative of mine, had examined them,' she said later. 'When I asked for them afterwards, all were missing. They had suddenly disappeared, supposedly having been sold by the workmen . . .'

Cantankerous and domineering, Dame Hoby eventually died at the age of 81, and although it does seem out of character, her restless spirit has haunted the Abbey ever since, weeping and mourning.

In the late 19th century, Admiral Edward Vansittart, a tough, no-nonsense sailor, had one of the most chilling experiences of Bisham Abbey's famous ghost. He had been playing chess with his brother late one night in the panelled room where the Dame's portrait hung. 'We had finished playing, and my brother had gone up to bed,' he once recalled. 'I stood for some time with my back to the wall, turning over the day in my mind. Minutes passed. I suddenly became aware of the presence of someone standing behind me. I spun round – it was Dame Hoby! And the frame on the wall was empty! Terrified, I fled from the room.'

Does anyone still see her, or hear her footsteps or echoes of unexplained crying in the night? Probably with all the cheerful bustle and noise upstairs and down at Bisham Abbey nowadays, even Dame Hoby goes unnoticed.

BRISTOL, BATH & AVON

The Phantom of Brockley Combe

Brockley Combe, in the Woodspring district of Avon, is an enchanting wooded valley and a favourite beauty spot for local people. Brockley Wood now boasts a Nature Trail and during the day when the sun is twinkling through the leaves of the tall trees it is difficult to imagine a more delightful place. But as dusk falls, visitors are glad to leave the Combe. This primitive woodland takes on a totally different character at night and, it is believed, harbours a ghost.

At the beginning of last century at a country inn near Brockley, the landlord was entertaining his customers with a story about a group of gypsies. It seems that they had been spending the night in the Combe when they had heard the sound of a heavy vehicle coming along the track at a great speed. Approaching them they saw a black coach, or hearse, drawn by four black horses. As the coach drew near they saw to their astonishment that the driver had no head! Terrified, the gypsies had fled from the Combe and had not returned there since.

As the landlord ended his tale, amid the 'oohs' and 'aahs' of the listeners, one man scoffed. 'Ghosts,' he declared, 'there ain't no such thing,' and just to show his contempt for the story he let it be known that when he left the inn that night he would walk home through the Combe. When the time came and the man took his leave, the other regulars looked at one another knowingly.

In the dead of night Brockley Combe is a silent, obscure place where the trees and rocks can take on weird forms in the moonlight. After the warmth and cheer of the inn, the man felt a little uneasy as he made his way along the dark track and began to wish that he had taken the main road home. Suddenly he heard coming towards him the sound of heavy wheels, hoof beats and strange voices. The man trembled and picked up a stone, reassuring himself all the time that ghosts were merely a figment of the imagination. From around the corner a vehicle appeared and instinctively the man threw the stone with all his might. The vehicle came violently to a halt. Just then the moon came out fully and he saw, to his amazement, that he had thrown a stone at a wagon containing the local football team, who were taking a short cut through the Combe on their way back from a victory celebration in a nearby village! The revellers shouted angrily at the man, for the stone had just missed hitting their driver. Full of high spirits – and cider – the lads decided to teach him a lesson. They jumped out of their wagon and started to chase him through the Combe.

He had hardly begun to run with the young men hard on his heels when, without warning, out of the darkness there appeared a huge, black hearse drawn by four snorting horses! This time it really was the phantom coach. They all witnessed it and froze with fear as it and its headless driver passed by.

Then it was gone. Silence returned. The football team raced back to their wagon and the driver set off at a cracking pace. As for the man from the inn, he ran home as fast as his legs would carry him without stopping for breath. For a week after the incident he was a nervous wreck and during the rest of his lifetime he never again ventured into Brockley Combe.

❖

Grey Ladies and Butterflies in Bath

It seems in keeping with Bath's Regency elegance that two of its most famous ghosts are charming rather than alarming. The Theatre Royal and the Garrick's Head pub next door share a Grey Lady who divides her appearances between them, leaving behind a delightful fragrance of jasmine.

Tradition says she was an actress who fell in love with an actor whom her husband challenged to a duel. The actor was killed, and his heartbroken lover took her own life. Her unseen presence is sometimes announced by an icy drop in temperature, but she has also been seen occupying a box at the theatre, sitting alone in her grey dress, wearing grey feathers in her hair and long white gloves.

Many actors performing at the Royal Theatre have noticed her, such as Liza Goddard and Christopher Timothy, and

The haunted box at Bath's Theatre Royal

Dame Anna Neagle and the cast of *The Dame of Sark* saw her in August 1975. And a stagehand setting the stage once reported that he looked up and saw the Grey Lady walking straight through the lines of seats in the Circle. He rushed up there, but there was no sign of anyone, just a pleasant scent of jasmine perfume!

Something uncanny happened just before a run of Noel Coward's play *Blithe Spirit*. As a publicity stunt, a mock séance was held on stage to promote the play, and it was a shock when the medium involved actually started to receive messages, apparently from the spirit of an 18th century actress. She said that she once starred at the theatre and had fallen in love with an actor, who had been killed when her husband challenged him to a duel. The listeners heard weeping as the voice told them that in her grief she had hung herself in her dressing room.

Had they unwittingly contacted the mysterious Grey Lady?

Apparently she is not content with just appearing from time to time, she sometimes wants to take part too. In June 1963 a clock was a necessary prop used in the play, and at an appropriate moment the stage lights dimmed without anyone touching them, and the clock chimed loudly three times. Strange, especially as the clock's mechanism had been removed!

The theatre also has a tradition concerning a butterfly. In 1938 the pantomime included a butterfly ballet, so it was an odd coincidence when a real one was found on stage. Sadly it was dead, and everyone thought it significant when the theatre manager died suddenly shortly afterwards. But as the show opened another butterfly, alive this time, appeared backstage and the panto was a big success.

Then some years later when Leslie Crowther starred in the Christmas panto a butterfly fluttered on stage and settled on his coat during rehearsal. It was carefully rescued, and the show broke all records! And so a superstition was born that a live butterfly was a lucky omen.

In December 2000 the pantomime was Cinderella, and on the first day of rehearsals the theatre's public relations man, Scott Rogers, woke to find the image of a butterfly had appeared in the condensation on his bedroom window. He casually rubbed it off, but it reappeared, and in spite of cleaning the window inside and out he could not get rid of the butterfly's image, and later on the 19th December a second butterfly shape joined it! And yes, the panto was a success!

BUCKINGHAMSHIRE

The Poisoner's Tale

No calendar of Buckinghamshire would be complete without a picture of the white-timbered watermill at Hambleden, mirrored in the river Thames. Alison Uttley called it the most beautiful place in the Thames Valley, and indeed the whole area of the Hambleden Valley includes some of the most delightful villages in the Chilterns, Turville, Fingest, Skirmett and Frieth.

One of Turville's claims to fame, apart from its picturesque charm, is a 19th century Rip Van Winkle remembered as the Sleeping Girl of Turville, who slumbered for a period variously described as seven or nine years. She lived in a cottage near the church known as Sleepy House, and was a constant source of interest to people who came from far and wide to see her. Her devoted mother kept her nourished, using a teapot to feed her with port wine and sugar. Apparently her mother died after a fall downstairs and not long afterwards her daughter awoke from her long nap, got married and had children. One wonders if her extended sleep could possibly have been nothing more than a drunken stupor due to too much port?

The Hambleden Valley area claims another famous character as a local ghost. Mary Blandy, the 18th century woman hung for poisoning her father, used to visit Turville Court, and Churchfield Wood must have been a favourite spot for a ride, as her ghost on a white horse has been seen there. One can imagine that she may have found solace in her lifetime in this beautiful place as she pondered her problems with the unreliable Captain Cranstoun and his 'love philtres' that were to lead her to the scaffold.

Mary Blandy seems to be an active ghost, as local people say she has often been seen walking down the lane that leads to Dolsden Farm, which would have been a bridlepath in her day. Elizabeth Wiltshire, who has made an interesting collection of ghost stories of the valley, tells of her grandfather's encounter with Mary Blandy's ghost one clear moonlit night.

The lane up from Dolsden Farm is steep and Wilfred Wiltshire was pushing his bicycle along there when he noticed someone approaching. In the bright moonlight he could see that it was a woman in strangely old-fashioned clothes and, as she got nearer, he could hear the rustle of her skirts. Because it was late for a woman to be out alone, he thought that she might be frightened at meeting a man in that lonely lane and he did not acknowledge her presence as they drew level. Then, deciding it might have been more reassuring if he had raised his cap and said 'Goodnight', he turned, but to his alarm, although he could still hear the rustle of her skirt, the figure had vanished! He hurried home, white and shaken, and told his wife: 'I've just seen a ghost.'

Other people have had a similar uncanny experience in the same area. In *The Buckinghamshire Dialect*, H. Harman recounts another first-hand report by a Turville resident. 'One dark night my wife and I were walking down the road ... we saw something pass us and heard the rustling of a silk dress. My wife nearly fainted ... I turned to see what it was, but could see nothing. It really upset my wife, and she has never forgotten it.'

Mary Blandy lived just over the border in Henley, where her father was a solicitor and the Town Clerk. Francis Blandy was a busy and prosperous man, ambitious that his only child, Mary, born in 1720, should make a happy and successful marriage. With this in mind he made no attempt to discount rumours that Mary's future inheritance would be in the region of £30,000. So Mary was considered quite a 'catch', although she was no beauty. In fact, although she had a good figure and striking black eyes, her face was described as 'rather ordinary, not improved by the results of smallpox.'

Francis Blandy intended that Mary's future husband should be something better than the local talent provided, and he and his wife

Mary Blandy, 'the notorious poisoner'

took Mary to Bath, as many parents with marriageable daughters did in those days.

There Mary proved to be quite a success, and she attracted several candidates for her hand. As we know from Jane Austen's descriptions of the social scene at Bath, there was nothing like a gallant soldier to set female hearts a-flutter, and Mary formed an attachment to one of her beaux, a captain, who was unfortunately ordered abroad with his regiment almost immediately.

However, this was a love match never destined to reach fulfilment, as fate in the shape of one Captain William Henry Cranstoun was waiting in the wings.

In the summer of 1746, Mary and her parents were invited to dinner at Paradise House, the home of General Mark Kerr. Captain Cranstoun, in Henley on a recruiting mission, was staying with the General and he and Mary were mutually attracted. Cranstoun must have had a charm of manner which did not rely on his physical appearance, as he is described as being short and ordinary looking, with sandy hair, small, weak eyes, a freckled and pitted skin, and 'clumsy legs'. He was known to have a roving eye, but to Mr and Mrs Blandy he was highly eligible due to the fact that he was the fifth son of a Scots peer, Lord Cranstoun.

During the summer of 1747, when Cranstoun again visited Henley, he declared his love for Mary. Although he made a casual reference to a Scottish lady who he said was falsely claiming to be his wife, Mary accepted his proposal. Her parents welcomed him with open arms and he came to stay with them for a time.

But Nemesis in the shape of a letter from a relative of Cranstoun's soon followed. It informed Mr Blandy that Cranstoun already had a wife and child in Scotland, having married Anne Murray in 1744. As she was a Jacobite and a Roman Catholic, the alliance had been kept secret lest it damaged his chances of promotion.

Mr Blandy was furious, but Mary and her mother believed Cranstoun's protestations that there would soon be an annulment. Attempts to get the marriage contract put aside failed, however, and the court declared Cranstoun legally married. He was, moreover, ordered to pay his wife an annuity, an unwelcome outcome he kept to himself.

Mrs Blandy's health deteriorated, and in September 1749 she died. Cranstoun had lost an ally and Mr Blandy now became increasingly unfriendly towards Cranstoun, and made no secret of the fact that his visits to the house were unwelcome.

Cranstoun told Mary about a wise woman he knew in Scotland whose 'love powders' acted like magic, and promised that if she gave some to her father they would make him more amenable to their relationship. Mary had her doubts, but later she recalled that one day, when her father was in a particularly angry mood, Cranstoun put some of his magic powder into Mr Blandy's tea and the old man became much more cheerful. This convinced her that her plausible lover could be right after all.

Cranstoun returned to Scotland early in 1751, from where he sent Mary some of the 'love philtres' to give to her father, with the result that Mr Blandy became very ill with pain and sickness. Their maid, Susan, happened to taste a cup of tea intended for Mr Blandy and was ill for a week afterwards. And, on another occasion, the family's old charwoman drank some of his tea, with similar results.

On 5th August 1751, Mary gave her father some gruel for his supper and he became so ill in the night that they had to call the apothecary. Next day, poor Mr Blandy was given more gruel, with the same results. And, later, when the cook brought the remains of his supper downstairs, the charwoman ate it and became violently sick.

When Mary wanted to give her father more of the same gruel, the maid protested that it was now too stale. She and the cook were becoming suspicious, and when they examined the gruel pan, they discovered some white, gritty substance at the bottom. They hid the pan in a locked cupboard overnight.

Mary's uncle, the Reverend Stevens, arrived on 9th August, and Susan told him about their suspicions. Next day they told Mr Blandy they thought he was being poisoned. Even so, the old man trustingly drank the tea Mary gave him at breakfast, simply complaining that it had a gritty taste.

In the light of these events, it is hard to believe that Mary did not know the true nature of Cranstoun's powders. The fact that Susan and the cook were eyeing her with suspicion was not lost on her, and she took Cranstoun's letters and what was left of the powder and threw them on the kitchen fire. With great presence of mind, the cook immediately put some more coal on the fire and, when Mary had gone, was able to rescue the paper packet still containing some of the white substance.

Meanwhile, Mr Blandy was deteriorating fast and the doctor had no doubt that his patient had been poisoned. When he left, he took with him the sediment from the gruel pan and the packet the cook had rescued from the fire.

Mr Blandy died on 14th August 1741, forgiving his daughter and warning her yet again about the treacherous Cranstoun. Too late, Mary Blandy realised what she had done and, full of remorse, she ran from the house, down Hart Street and over the bridge to the Angel Inn. But angry Henley residents followed her there, and she was taken to Oxford where she was tried for murder on 29th February 1752.

She was found guilty and hanged on 6th April 1752, protesting her innocence to the end. After her death, Mary's body was brought back to Henley and buried at night between the graves of her parents in the presence of an enormous crowd of local people. Was it just curiosity that brought them there, or did they see her not as a murderer but rather as an innocent girl used by a heartless villain?

Cranstoun himself did not live long after her. On 2nd December in the same year he died at Furnes, near Dunkirk, of a strange illness which caused him to expire in great agony. He was 46 years old.

With such a history, Mary Blandy's return to her former haunts as a ghost seems not unexpected, and over the years any unexplained apparition within range of Henley was automatically claimed to be the notorious poisoner.

The Blandy home in Hart Street, Henley was later demolished and another house built on the site, but sometimes Mary's ghost is said to stand beneath an old mulberry tree at the end of the garden.

In 1969 she made a dramatic appearance at the Kenton Theatre in Henley. *The Hanging Wood*, a play by Joan Morgan, based on Mary Blandy's story, was in rehearsal at the theatre when people began to notice various odd happenings. Doors would open by themselves, then slam shut suddenly, and lights came on and off without human intervention. Then the cast noticed the figure of a woman standing at the back of the theatre watching the rehearsals. Whenever anyone approached her, however, she faded away into the shadows and was gone. Miss Morgan remembered that some years before, when a dramatised version of Mary Blandy's trial was performed at Henley Town Hall, a similar figure had been seen at the back of the hall while they were rehearsing.

Was it the ghost of Mary Blandy herself? Naturally, members of the cast thought so, and one evening as they sat drinking coffee and talking about her, something happened to convince any sceptics. Someone had placed a cup on the floor and, as the cast watched in amazement, it rose right up for several inches, and then was dashed down again to break into pieces.

Until recently, there was apparently no known portrait of Mary Blandy in her home town, but in 1987 the Hon Georgina Stonor discovered a print of her, which she presented to the town the following year. One must admit that, if this is a true likeness, Mary has a cool and calculating stare, and her heavily lidded eyes appear to view the world with deep suspicion. Surely a woman like that would have recognised that Cranstoun's love philtres were nothing other than the deadly poison, arsenic?

Was Mary Blandy guilty or was she innocent after all? Who can say, but it seems her spirit is still restless.

CAMBRIDGESHIRE

College Ghosts

Jesus College

C ambridge University is almost 800 years old and many of its colleges are reputed to be haunted, including Jesus College founded in 1496 by John Alcock, Bishop of Ely. Its oldest buildings formed part of a nunnery built circa 1133 and dedicated to the virgin St Radegund. Leading from the stone floor in the angle of the cloister adjoining the Hall is an extremely steep staircase formerly called 'Cow Lane', now 'G' staircase. This is the route to the infamous 'Ghost Room', which following the last meeting of the Everlasting Club held there on 2nd November 1766 was considered unfit for human habitation and remained firmly padlocked for some 200 years.

This club, modelled on the Hellfire Club, was founded in the 18th century by the Hon Alan Dermot, the hedonistic son of an Irish peer. Membership was both corporeal and incorporeal (in life and death) and limited to seven: himself, Charles Bellasis, Henry Davenport, Francis Witherington, James Harvey, William Catherston and one other. The behaviour of these 'Everlastings' aged between 22 and 30 years was totally degenerate. One was a Fellow-Commoner of Trinity, three were Fellows of other colleges, another a Fellow of Jesus College, one a landed gentleman and the seventh a Cambridge physician.

Between 1738 and 1743 accounts of their meetings were recorded in a minute book, in which each member signed his name and entered his address. Arthur Gray, Master of Jesus from 1912 to 1940, included the story of the club in his anthology of college ghosts, and said that although this book came into the possession of a predecessor, it probably no longer exists.

The entrance gateway to Jesus College, Cambridge

The Annual Meeting, the most degenerate event of the year, was held at 10 pm every All Souls' Day, the 2nd November, with each member taking his turn to host the event in his place of residence. When the high-spirited Alan Dermot signed the book on 2nd November 1743 his companions were completely unaware that five days earlier he had been killed in a duel in Paris, and according to the rules was now an incorporeal member! When they realised they had been roistering with a ghost, 'they left Cambridge and buried themselves in widely parted regions.' None wished to continue with the Annual Meeting, but were obliged by the club rules to meet every October to put their objection in writing.

Over the next 23 years all except Charles Bellasis died, and on 18th May 1766 he recorded in the minute book that he was the only remaining corporeal member. Now a sober Fellow of Jesus College, with the scandal of his younger days unknown to the new generation of students and long forgiven by his contemporaries, he lived in the college at the top of the 'Cow Lane' staircase. Although he was alone in his room on the night of 2nd November that year, at 10 pm all hell broke loose. For two hours many heard the sound of crashing glass, breaking furniture, bawdy songs, swearing and blaspheming. Not even the Master dared to enter Bellasis' chamber. However, peace returned at midnight, and when workmen eventually smashed the lock on the sturdy oak door the following morning they discovered seven chairs placed around the table. Six were overturned, and in the other sat the remaining 'Everlasting', who was dead.

That night the final entry had been made in the minute book. Six 'Everlastings' had signed their names, but none had given their addresses.

Although this room was turned into a store and remained locked and disused for almost two centuries, at 10 pm on All Souls' Day (a time traditionally associated with ghosts and spirits) the raucous din of the 'Everlastings' could be heard from behind its stout door. Then there was peace and in 1924 the room was converted back into living quarters and has been corporeally occupied ever since.

Corpus Christi College

F ounded in 1352, this is one of the smallest and oldest of the Cambridge colleges. One of several Corpus Christi ghosts is said to be that of the gentle Dr Butts, Vice-Chancellor of the University who became the Master of Corpus Christi in 1626.

In 1630 Cambridge was beset by plague and Dr Butts wrote to Lord Coventry, High Steward of Cambridge, describing the plight of the town, for which as a principal figure, he felt a large share of responsibility. Butts became more and more dejected and on Easter Day, 1st April 1632 the

Corpus Christi College

pulpit in Great Mary's church from which he always preached stood empty. Aware of his depression, a frantic search was made of Corpus Christi and he was found hanging by the neck in his rooms above the kitchens in Old Court. For many years following his suicide his ghost was seen, with a huge red gash about its neck, haunting these very rooms. It was always at a time when a college member was either seriously ill or in extreme danger.

Another spectre, also reputed to be of that period, is that of Elizabeth, the daughter of Dr William Spencer, Rector of Landbeach near Cambridge and Master of Corpus Christi from the 1630s to 1693.

For several years young Elizabeth had been embroiled in a secret love affair, using the kitchens in the old Lodge as a trysting place. One day the lovers were disturbed. With no time to spare she hid her paramour in a wooden chest, where he died of suffocation. We are not told when she died, but her death was not peaceful. Elizabeth Spencer haunted these rooms until their conversion into living quarters in 1825, frightening any servants who were working after dark.

A curious incident which allegedly occurred in rooms opposite these former kitchens was reported in an article in the *Occult Review* of March 1905, as quoted by Edith Porter in her book *Cambridgeshire Customs and Folklore.*

'In the Easter term of 1904 an undergraduate … who had rooms opposite those said to be haunted, happened to come in at three o'clock in the afternoon, and as soon as he had sat down to work, found himself seized with a curious feeling of uneasiness, which made it impossible for him to concentrate his mind. He got up and, looking out of the window, noticed the head and shoulders of a man leaning out of the window of the upper set of rooms opposite. The features, he was rather surprised to find, he could not recognise: they were those of a stranger with long hair, who remained perfectly motionless, and seemed to glare down upon him. For three minutes he stood at the window and watched, and then, thinking he might see better from his bedroom, he ran there, but by the time he had arrived, the man opposite had completely disappeared.

'The young man was now thoroughly excited and went across the court to the upper set of rooms opposite. However, he found the door locked, and when he called no answer was given. In the evening, after careful enquiry, he discovered that the owner of the rooms had been out the whole afternoon, and that it was quite impossible that anyone could have been in the rooms from the time of his departure at two o'clock to the arrival of his bedmaker at half-past six.'

After the apparition had been seen again on subsequent occasions the occupier of the rooms 'made up his mind to try to exorcise it, and got C——, a friend from another college, who was interested in spiritualism, to come to his rooms for the purpose, with four other men.

'At the outset they all knelt down, said the Lord's Prayer, and called upon the Three Persons of the Trinity to command the spirit to appear. It was then seen, but only by two of the six men. Another said that he felt a peculiarly cold and chilling air, but the rest saw nothing. The two who saw the ghost – the man interested in spiritualism and the occupant of the rooms – describe it as appearing in the form of a mist of about a yard wide, which slowly developed into the form of a man who seemed to be shrouded in white, and had a gash in his neck, and that it then moved slowly about the room. The two men got up, and, holding the crucifix in front of them, approached the apparition, but seemed to be forced back by some invisible agency. They cried out, "It drives me back", and then both completely broke down, becoming quite unnerved.

'A few days later they tried to exorcise the spirit, with exactly the same result; the same men saw it, and no one else. They were again driven back, although this time they approached holding hands. The others allege that they appeared to grow stiff, and that they gripped one another convulsively. The meeting was again broken up without anything definite having been effected.'

Geoff Yeates gives a fuller and more chilling account in his book *Cambridge College Ghosts*. Several undergraduates witnessed the commotion which accompanied the exorcism and he says the college authorities tried to hush things up and temporarily closed the haunted rooms. It took an American who struck a deal to live in them rent free to restore the status quo, even it if did not stop the Sunday trippers from congregating under the notorious windows, hoping to catch a glimpse of the ghostly occupant.

CHESHIRE

Hauntings, Human and Animal – and Feathered

G odley Green, now considered part of Hyde, has a remarkable history of hauntings for such a small area. One of the old stone-built farmhouses, looking out over Matley and Hattersley, had a long-running history of mysterious happenings.

It was once owned by a farming family, the last survivor of which was an old dame whose nose and chin almost met. As so often happened in those days, stories began to attach themselves to this strange-looking old lady. In still earlier times, she would probably have been considered a witch, but in her day – the later 18th century – she attracted the doubtless gossip-worthy rumour that a vast treasure lay buried in or near the farm. And when her ghost began to appear after her death, wandering erratically through the farm at night, it was immediately assumed that she was looking for her treasure. Doors – even locked doors – were mysteriously and suddenly opened, other doors locked themselves. Beds were rocked violently and bedclothes snatched off the sleepers. Fire-irons, pots and pans rattled, and there was a noise like that of a floor being swept.

During the early and middle 19th century, these occurrences were so frequent that the occupants came to accept them and took no notice of them. But in 1880 two children, who had been left alone in the house, heard a strange noise in an upstairs room and went to investigate. On opening the door to one room, they were confronted by an old rocking chair, swinging to and fro as if there were someone sitting in it. A farm labourer, frantically summoned, was too terrified of the sight to attempt to stop it, and finally the farmer's wife actually sat in it to still the movement. It was believed that the old woman had died in that chair.

Also, there was a certain part of the garden where nothing would grow, whatever was done in the way of gardening. Bones had been dug up there at some earlier time, and it is possible that they had something to do with the continued sterility of the ground.

In the early years of the 20th century, somewhere about 1906, the then tenant's wife left home to go on an errand to Gee Cross, leaving her brother ill at home. On her return, accompanied by her mother, the evening was fine and still, with no sounds other than birdsong, and no wind. Suddenly, in front of them, a high thorn hedge started to rock violently, and from behind it there appeared, from the direction of the farm, an apparently female figure dressed in white. And when, a few moments later, the tenant's wife reached the farm, she discovered that her brother had just died.

Another old lady also made her regular appearances at Godley Green, so much so that the locals barely noticed her. Dressed in an old-fashioned cap, and with kilted-up skirt and apron, she would appear shaking the apron and making a peculiar hissing noise – conceivably chasing geese, but who knows? On one such occasion she was seen by a small group of visitors, who were accompanied by a relative of the old lady. 'Oh, it's owd Nancy reet enough,' he said with a touch of annoyance. 'Why the Devil can't she rest quiet in her grave? What does she want frightening people like that?'

One of Cheshire's many animal ghosts also appeared at Godley Green on several occasions. This spectral hound was described as being 'as big as a cow', with huge, yellow, staring eyes, lolling tongue and foaming mouth. It gave out a terrifying, sepulchral baying. It appeared suddenly one night on the road, in the early years of the last century, next to a homegoing wanderer, keeping steady pace with him, always watching him unblinkingly. The man struck at it, and his hand went clean through it and was scratched by the hedge on the other side. Afterwards, he said: 'It was the most hideous thing I ever saw. Its feet went pit-a-pat, pit-a-pat, with a horrible clanking noise like chains. I wouldn't meet it again for twenty pounds. I never want to see it again if I live to be a hundred!'

Then there was the endearing – not to say eccentric – duck in Stanney, which appeared in a lane outside the village and pecked at passing ankles. Attempts by the village parson to exorcise the duck by conventional methods failed miserably – presumably because the duck didn't know it was being exorcised – and finally, in desperation, the village butcher took matters into his own hands. Arming himself with his cleaver, he lay in wait for the duck and managed to behead it, burying the head in the ditch at the top of Stoak Lane.

Leaving aside the question of how you behead an intangible bird, it sadly has to be recorded that the butcher was only half-successful: thereafter the lane was still haunted – but by a headless duck!

❖

Haunted Hostelries

I had thought that only Cheshire could boast a ghost duck; but it is even odder than that. It actually boasts *two* ghost ducks!

The Blue Bell Inn at Tushingham once had a pet duck. Doubtless it started out as a cute, fluffy little thing adored by all and sundry, but it grew up to be distinctly misanthropic. Of course, this is understandable enough: no self-respecting duck would relish a life of being accidentally kicked in a crowded bar, having ale splashed over it, and probably being half-choked by clouds of tobacco smoke into the bargain. In the end it rebelled and turned to pecking at so many intruding ankles that it was at last reluctantly killed by the landlord. However, he was apparently sufficiently soft-hearted not to eat an erstwhile family pet; instead the duck was interred beneath the bottom step of the stairs going down to the cellar.

That should have been the end of the story, but the duck clearly hadn't yet had all the revenge it wanted. Regularly thereafter, the step would come loose, no matter how firmly down it was nailed, and the duck would emerge, to reappear upstairs, pecking away to its heart's content.

In the end, the landlord turned to the church, and the local parson arranged a praying-down ceremony. Seven parsons are the minimum required for a praying-down, but this parson was nothing if not thorough and, with an enthusiasm that can only be described as overkill for one little duck, rounded up no fewer than twelve. Things didn't go quite according to plan, though, for instead of returning to its grave under the stairs, the duck remained where it was. But gradually it started to shrink. With a sudden flash of genius, the local parson waited until the wretched bird was small enough, and then shoved it into an empty bottle, hastily jamming the cork tightly in. The bottle was bricked up in a wall, and peace returned once again to the Blue Bell.

More recently, when the pub was undergoing repairs, the bottle was carefully removed from its hole, and later sealed back into the new wall. Clearly even today no one is taking any chances.

The Orange Tree pub at Altrincham has two ghosts – a screaming girl, and a monk in the cellar, and sometimes the sound of Latin chanting can be heard passing through the cellar and on through the wall, as if a procession of monks is going by. One wonders if the screaming girl encountered the monks?

The Halfway House at Childer Thornton dates back to 1753 and has long had a reputation for being haunted, and so when a local radio crew thought a Hallowe'en broadcast from the pub would be a good idea, the Halfway House was the obvious choice.

The equipment was set up and all was ready on the night but just as they were about to broadcast live, they found that there were all kinds of problems with their equipment, the mikes weren't working, the earpieces were dead, and the aerial fell down for no apparent reason.

Then the real ale pump wouldn't work and when the landlord went down to the cellar he found beer all over the floor. He returned to the bar to find that the pump was now working normally, but when he went back to the cellar he found mayhem – the beer pumps were turning themselves on and off and the lights, too, were switching on and off with no one near them!

When he and some of the crew went back upstairs they saw the figure of an old lady in a white apron standing in the hall at the top of the stairs. Enquiries later divulged that a previous landlady who fitted the description was in the habit of standing there to keep her eye on the bar, lounge and cellar!

Ye Olde Number Three pub at Little Bollington was an old coaching inn, and inevitably had its own unseen 'regular'. One interested ghost-hunter was there one day and when the landlord described the time when the resident poltergeist threw a large mirror at him, he unwisely expressed amused disbelief. Immediately his glass of beer rose in the air, moved along and crashed to the floor! The investigator was equally shattered, and also convinced now that there genuinely was something there!

He asked if he could spend the night in the pub after closing time, and the landlord agreed, but pointed out that whatever might happen was at the investigator's own risk. Nothing happened for a time, and at about 1.30 am he went to the bar for a few minutes, but when he returned to the lounge, he found that in the meantime two stools had moved to block the doorway. Later he decided to have a sandwich and some coffee, and suddenly a large glass case kept behind the bar containing cigars rose up and crashed down on the table in front of him, smashing his thermos flask! The rest of the night remained peaceful – obviously the pub's ghost felt it had made its point.

CORNWALL

Parson Dodge to the Rescue!

O ver two centuries ago, humble folk lived in fear and dread of the
spirit world, and sought some means of protection from such ills.
Recognising that need in Cornwall, there was no shortage of parsons
keen to demonstrate their influence over these spirits; a situation which
fed superstition and helped the men of the cloth gain a tighter control
over their innocent flocks.

Life was particularly hard for the rural folk in Cornwall, who had
traditionally enjoyed the rights of common land to help them eke out a
frugal existence by growing their own vegetables, keeping a few animals
and hunting wild game for the pot. But human nature being what it is,
certain greedy landowners sought to enclose the common land and claim
it as their own without due regard for anyone else. Indeed, in the 17th
century two wealthy landowners were in bitter dispute with each other
about the acquisition of the common near Lanreath, in East Cornwall. The
matter was taken to court, and the situation was so fraught with animosity
that the loser flew into a violent rage and died. Few mourned his passing,
but many were to fear his antics from beyond the grave.

When it comes to being preoccupied with the material things of this
life, the philosophical might subscribe to the theory that 'you can't take it
with you'. But this ambitious loser apparently reckoned that he would
have a good try, or at least ensure that no one else would enjoy it. The
artful old devil returned to haunt the common! He appeared as a black
apparition driving a phantom carriage across the moors, drawn by a team
of headless horses and generally creating pandemonium. Local folk
going home across the moors took to their heels in terror. The news
spread like wildfire, gaining additional, dramatic details in the telling,
until the entire population reached a state of panic. 'We'll go to the vicar,'

'Dodge is come! I must be gone!' says the spectre

they said. 'He's a man of the cloth who understands these things. He'll know what to do.' So they went to the vicar.

The mild-mannered vicar of Lanreath listened to their stories, which seemed to get more and more outrageous, and did his best to reassure them, but they demanded action. And so it was that the sexton of Lanreath found himself on his way to Parson Dodge at his vicarage in the village of Talland, bearing a note from the vicar of Lanreath, requesting help in resolving a disturbing situation which was terrifying his parishioners. He had heard about Parson Dodge, who was celebrated in dealing with such problems; everybody had heard about the old parson and his colourful exploits with fiendish spirits, for his fame had spread far and wide.

The old, grey vicarage with its heavy chimneys, graceful gables and mellow, mullioned windows lurked in those days behind high walls, trees and shrubs, providing an apt setting for one with such a reputation. The sexton nervously tied up his trusty horse, opened the squeaky gate and lifted the big brass knocker on the hefty oak door. A young servant girl tripped along to open it, and asked him to come inside. Whereupon he was shown along dark, dank passages and into the sunless parlour where the great man sat, looking scholarly and thoughtful. As the reverend gentleman looked at the letter he was clearly startled, but as he read and reread the letter, he assumed an air of coolness and mastery. 'Er ... Yes. Are the villagers really as frightened as this letter would imply?' he inquired, in matter-of-fact tones. 'If you please, Sir, they be truly terrified. Folks doesn't sleep well in their beds o' nights for fear of the evil spirit. An' every night it do seem to git nearer. 'Fore long 'twill be in the village, an' then wot shall us do?' The vicar questioned the sexton closely as to the nature of the strange phenomenon. 'I ain't seen one o' those, but I see'd the ghost an' is 'eadless 'orses an' the carriage wot rides across the sky o' nights ... Well, not acherly *see'd*. But we 'eard 'un! Me an' my good lady, we 'eard un! We 'eard all the c'mmotion an' the racin' wheels. "Ghostly coach wheels, they be," I says to me good wife, an' she be that afear'd. Please, yer Reverence, you be the one us do need. Everyone do know as 'ow sprits be terrified o' Parson Dodge. Please 'elp we.' If the modest parson felt his ego being inflated, he did his best not to show it. 'Pray, tell your vicar that I'm busy tomorrow, but will come over to Lanreath the following evening,' he declared evenly, before turning his attentions to other matters.

Two nights later Parson Dodge and the vicar of Lanreath set off for the moor on horseback to investigate the haunting. If the moor looked somewhat bleak and inhospitable on a winter's day, it looked decidedly more so on a winter's night, as eerie winds whistled around the trees and isolated homesteads, and swept across the open wasteland, carrying with it the dismal sounds of dogs baying in the distance. Although uneasy, each adopted a certain air of bravado, to impress the other, and to convince themselves of their unswerving trust in the Divine. They bravely patrolled the bleak and lonely landscape and looked for sinister signs, but nothing seemed to be brewing.

With mixed relief and disappointment, they decided to abandon the attempt. 'It was good of you to have come,' said the parson of Lanreath. 'We'll try again some other time,' replied his ghost-laying colleague. 'We'll choose a night that's more conducive to spirits; the sort of night that draws them to their former haunts.' So saying, they each departed their separate ways, for the vicar of Lanreath made straight for his rectory, while Mr Dodge tried a short cut back to Talland.

Parson Dodge's old grey mare ambled amiably along the track until they reached the valley bottom near Blackadon, when she began to show signs of distress. She stared whinneying, then came to a halt and refused to go any further. When her master attempted to urge her forwards, she moved backwards, and when he dug in his spurs and lashed with his whip, she became more frightened, pranced about and threw up her haunches. He dismounted and tried to lead her gently forward by the reins, but she would not have it. He remounted and tried to proceed, but she refused to move forward. When he dropped the reins, she backed, turned around and retraced their route.

In shades of darkness the profile of the moor seemed to be altering. The mare became distressed as changing, indefinable shapes became more menacing, until they took on the form of the fearful, black spectre with his coach and headless horses. Then Parson Dodge beheld the ghostly driver, whip in hand standing over a cowering person on the ground, which could only be his fellow parson. With cool head and iron nerve, our celebrated layer-of-ghosts summoned up a prayer, but before he could give it utterance, the fearful spectre became aware of a superior presence and exclaimed, 'Dodge is come! I must be gone!' (Or at least, that is what the good man reported later.) Whereupon he leapt into his carriage and disappeared beyond the dark horizon.

In the meantime the other horse had taken flight and bolted, and the folk of Lanreath were awakened by the clattering sound of horse's hooves. Some panicked, thinking this was the arrival of the phantom come to haunt them; others recognised it as the vicar's horse, and realised that something was amiss. So they set off for the moor, where they found their vicar senseless in the arms of Parson Dodge. The victim's eyelids began to flicker, but he was in such a state of shock that he had to be carried home by his parishioners. Happily the adventure ended here, for the incoherent clergyman soon recovered from his ordeal and returned to the pulpit to preach the Good Word to his flock. And as for the phantom mischief-maker, neither he, his headless horses nor his coach were ever seen again.

❖

St Nectan's Glen

When I was in my teens my friend Doris and I spent a holiday in Cornwall at the home of a family friend. We were staying at Trethevy, not far from Tintagel, and on our first evening we couldn't wait to explore, so set off after supper with the dog.

We'd seen a small wooden sign pointing to 'The Kieve', and having no idea what a Kieve was, we went to find out. We found ourselves in a leafy glen with a stream running through it, and continued along the narrow path to the end where there was a beautiful waterfall. Our little dog was enjoying himself running about and we found what seemed to be a small tea garden and some buildings at the end. It looked as if the only way back home was to return the way we had come, and there was no one about to ask.

The light was fading as we started back along the path, and with trees high on each side the glen had become quite shadowy. There seemed to be a different atmosphere now, hard to describe, and we fell silent. I noticed that we were walking faster, the little dog clinging to our heels.

Somehow I was neither surprised nor really frightened when I saw the figure on the opposite bank of the stream. Doris was looking straight ahead and I felt sure she hadn't seen it so I said nothing, but when I looked again the figure in a long monk-like robe was still there, not moving, but watchful.

We were almost running by the time we emerged from the glen and then we stopped. Just a few steps beyond the path the atmosphere had completely changed, and Doris looked at me, eyebrows raised. 'What was the matter with us?' she asked.

'I wanted to get out before they came,' I answered. 'They?' she queried. 'What do you mean?'

I knew I wasn't making sense. 'I don't know,' I said, 'I thought there would be a long line of them coming along the path towards us, and it was so narrow, I didn't want to be there when they came.'

When we arrived back at the bungalow where we were staying, Carol, our hostess, said, 'You two look as if you've seen a ghost! Where have you been?'

'To Nectan's Kieve,' we said.

'What? At night? Don't you know its haunted?'

Well, of course we didn't know, and if we had we'd probably have wanted to go there anyway. Carol had only lived at Trethevy for a short

St Nectan's Glen, for many years a place of pilgrimage

time but she told us that local people said that ghostly monks had been seen in the glen, and one night a boy from the village had met a long line of them walking along the path towards the waterfall.

I hadn't visited Nectan's Glen again until a few years ago when my husband and I were on holiday in Cornwall and found ourselves in the Trethevy area. I had discovered more about this mysterious place with its legendary saint since my previous visit and knew that Saint Nectan was reputed to have had his sanctuary just by the waterfall in the 6th century. From his tower he could see the sea, and would ring a bell to warn ships approaching the treacherous Cornish coast.

When he was near the end of his life, he cast his bell into the basin below the waterfall (the Kieve), and after his death, two women thought to be his sisters arrived. Tradition says they diverted the waterfall and in the riverbed below they buried an oak chest containing the saint's body, and various religious treasures. The river was then allowed to flow back, and the Saint's former hermitage became a place of pilgrimage for many years.

In the 19th century a cottage was built on the site, where the present bungalow and café now stand. On our visit, my husband and I had tea there and talked to the proprietor who agreed that people had encountered monks in the glen, and heard the sounds of chanting, and he said that a hooded figure had sometimes been seen in a grey habit, a gentle, kindly apparition. He also told us of the evening when he looked out of his kitchen window and saw a monk walking around his yard where he had a small aviary, apparently interested in his birds. One minute he was there, and the next he had vanished.

It is easy to believe such happenings in this strange and beautiful wooded glen with its rippling stream and the waterfall splashing down to the basin below where Saint Nectan is sleeping, and some say at times you can hear the sound of his silver bell.

CUMBRIA

Seeing Things

D o you believe in fairies? Jack Wilson of Martindale did. So did the clergy of Lamplugh, the folk of Little Langdale, Ravenglass, Stainton, Lanercost, Penrith and many another Cumbrian settlement. For them fairies were simply a fact of life.

Jack Wilson believed in them because he saw them and witnessed their departure, never to return. His account, recorded in 1857, tells how on a moonlit night, while crossing Sandwick Rigg, he came upon a large group of fairies dancing.

At first they didn't see him, so he crept closer. From their midst a ladder rose from the ground, disappearing into a cloud. Then the fairies spotted him and scurried up to the cloud, drawing their ladder up after them. 'Yance gane, ae gane, an' nivver saw mair o' them,' he said.

The presence of little creatures was also taken for granted in Lamplugh, where a page from what was apparently a register of deaths, 1st January 1658 to 1st January 1663, records: 'Frightened to death by fairies – three.' And at The Busk in Little Langdale, obliging fairies were said to churn the butter while the family slept.

Fairy Bead Beck, near Stainton, was so called because of its oddly-shaped pebbles, some of them resembling cups and saucers fit for fairies; and in Ravenglass everyone said that the local Roman remains had been the palace of King Eveling and his daughter, the fairy Modron.

In Lanercost folk spoke in the 1880s of hearing the jingle of fairies' horses' harness, and 20 years later a Lanercost resident recalled a present of butter, left by fairies for a ploughman. One of his horses ate it and flourished; the other rejected it and died.

The fairies disappear from Jack Wilson's view on Sandwick Rigg

All Penrith knew of the 'Luck' of the Musgraves, of nearby Eden Hall. This was an ancient, elaborately decorated glass chalice. Antiquarians expressed varying opinions on its provenance, but the account preferred had nothing to do with scholarship.

It was said that on a summer night one of the Hall's servants went to fetch water from St Cuthbert's Well, in the grounds. Nearby he saw fairies dancing around a glass beaker. Drawn to the goblet by its unusual design, he reached over the fairies and picked it up.

'If this cup should break or fall,' chanted the fairies, 'farewell the luck of Eden Hall.' So the chalice was thereafter kept carefully in a leather container. The Hall's luck ran out in 1934, when the Musgraves' home was demolished. But the 'Luck' itself – identified as a 13th century Syrian goblet, believed to have been acquired by a Musgrave during the Crusades – is preserved at the Victoria and Albert Museum.

Fairies could also be blamed when things went wrong. Thus, when bridge-building difficulties were encountered at Shap during the construction of the railway from Lancaster to Carlisle, fairies were convenient scapegoats. They could be relied upon to be elusive, like the one snapped by the Cumberland photographer W.B. Redmayne when he spotted it while birdwatching near Dalston. On developing his film he was dismayed to find that the sprite was nowhere to be seen ...

Yet another vanishing act was performed on Souther Fell, near Threlkeld. And this time it wasn't just a few fairies that disappeared. It was a whole army.

On Midsummer Eve in 1735, a farm servant, Daniel Stricket, was astonished to see troops marching across Souther Fell. They appeared to be well-disciplined, and for an hour he watched company after company pass across the fell and disappear over the top. Few believed his story ... until, two years later, again on Midsummer Eve, the spectacle was repeated. The army was on horseback, and this time it was witnessed by Stricket's employer, William Lancaster, and his family.

In 1743 a Wilton Hill farmer and one of his workers reported seeing a man and a dog on Souther Fell, chasing some horses. This didn't strike them as particularly unusual ... until the man, dog and horses all vanished without a sound, over a precipice. A search of the fell beneath the cliff failed to find any bodies.

All this, however, was merely a curtain raiser for what was to follow. On Midsummer Eve in 1745, the phantom army returned, its ranks interspersed this time with what appeared to be carriages, passing across terrain which was quite inaccessible to wheeled transport. The spectators on this occasion numbered some 26 witnesses, several of whom scoured the fell the next day for horseshoes, wheel-tracks and footprints, but found nothing. Yet they all knew what they had seen, saying they were prepared to swear to it before a magistrate; and 40 years later two survivors among them put their names to an attestation of what they had witnessed.

Those seeking a rational explanation spoke of mirages, of tricks performed by refractions of light – it was said that at the time of the 1745 illusion, rebel troops had been exercising on the south-west coast of Scotland. Others pointed out that Bonnie Prince Charlie didn't raise his standard until 19th August. They also noted that residents of the Souther Fell area had a reputation for credulity – there was a tradition that the reflection of stars could be seen at noon in the waters of Scales and Bowscale tarns, the latter being inhabited by two immortal fish.

Daniel Stricket, the first person to see the vanishing army, later became an auctioneer. Doubtless he pronounced 'Going, going, gone,' with rare conviction.

The Croglin Vampire

It was in 1874 that the Australian brothers Michael and Edward Cranswell and their sister Amelia rented Croglin Grange, in the Vale of Eden. Captain Fisher, their landlord, found them to be good tenants, and they became popular in the village. All went well until one summer night when Amelia went to bed without closing her shutters.

She slept soundly until something, she couldn't say what, awoke her. Going to her window, she was horrified when her gaze was met by two flaming eyes set in a hideous brown face.

The creature outside seemed to be human, but was swathed in shrouds. As it peered at her through the window, its shrivelled fingers scrabbled at the panes. Amelia had locked her door before retiring. Now she wished she hadn't, for in her panic to get out she fumbled at the lock and dropped the key.

Her screams roused her brothers. They broke open Amelia's door and stumbled into her room, to find her lying senseless on the floor. Her neck was bleeding, punctured by what appeared to be marks made by fangs. The brothers rushed to her now-open window, but there was no sign of her attacker.

Amelia's wounds were superficial and she soon regained consciousness, but the Cranswells felt that a temporary change of scene was needed. A long holiday in Switzerland would calm Amelia's shattered nerves, they decided, and they were right. On their return Amelia continued to occupy the same bedroom, although she now took care always to close the shutters at night and to leave the door unlocked. And the brothers kept a gun handy, just in case ...

The incident was all but forgotten when, months later, Amelia was woken by the sound of her shutters being forced. Her cries soon brought her brothers to her aid, and Edward dashed outside, gun in hand. He was just in time to see a wraith-like figure fleeing down the drive. He took a shot at it, and the creature stumbled but continued running.

Edward pursued it across frosty fields in the March moonlight and saw it enter Croglin churchyard, where it vanished among the graves. The brother went back to the Grange, returning after dawn to the churchyard, accompanied by several villagers. They discovered that a family vault had been opened. All the coffins inside except one had been disturbed, revealing their skeletal remains.

Opening the undamaged coffin, the searchers found the preserved form of the presumed vampire inside, with a bullet wound in one of its legs. It appeared to be in a coma, and nobody waited for it to come to life. Edward and his helpers lifted it from the coffin, carried it to a corner of the churchyard, built a fire and burned it.

The event was chronicled in the memoirs of Augustus Hare (1834-1903), who named Captain Fisher as his source. Sceptics have remarked that there is no Croglin Grange, and that Hare was noted for his susceptibility to the far-fetched. But there is a Croglin Low Hall ... where a ground-floor window has been walled up.

DERBYSHIRE

Dickey's Skull

An unusual ornament graces the windowsill of a farm at Tunstead, about two miles south-east of Whaley Bridge. It is a human skull, known as Dickey, and it is said to have been there for over 370 years. The skull is olive green, shaded at the edges with green and white spots. At one time it was possible to buy postcards bearing a photograph of it.

One story says that it is the skull of Trooper Ned Dickson, who fought in France during the Huguenot Wars. After fighting bravely at the Battle of Ivry, and saving the life of Lord Willoughby, Ned was badly wounded and lay on the field of battle all night. He was not expected to survive, but after a long period of convalescence, he eventually recovered. His health was too poor for him to remain a soldier and he returned to his farm in Tunstead. Here he found that his cousin, Jack Johnson, had taken possession of the property in the belief that Ned was dead. Jack and his wife greeted the reappearance of Ned Dickson with a lack of enthusiasm, but eventually invited him to stay the night at the farm. During the night, the treacherous cousin is said to have murdered Ned, cutting off his head with an axe while he slept. Jack and his wife buried the corpse, and went about their business as though Ned had never returned. Then, a few months after the murder, Jack's wife was horrified to see the gruesome sight of Ned's head standing upright on a stone in the farmhouse, 'as wan and as ghastly as when he was done'. The head remained with the couple for the rest of their lives, the skin and flesh rotting away to leave the skull.

Another story says that the skull was that of one of two co-heiresses who was murdered for her share of the inheritance. On her deathbed, she decreed that her bones should never be taken from the farm. After her death, the farmhouse was haunted by frightful noises for many years. These intensified until they were unbearable. At this point, the dying words of the woman were recalled, her bones were dug up and her skull placed on the farmhouse windowsill. This story seems to have more credence, since scientific tests have proved that Dickey is in fact female. Nevertheless, the masculine name has stuck. This has puzzled investigators for many years. In 1809 a local historian wrote, 'Why it should have been baptised with a name belonging to the male sex seems somewhat anomalous.'

The two legends agree on one thing, that if the skull is moved from the farm, then terrible consequences ensue. Not all the tenants of the farm have accepted this. Some have objected to having human remains in the house because it seemed disrespectful, while others have been scornful of the superstitions attached to the skull. In every case, however, these tenants have been forced to change their minds and have restored Dickey to his/her rightful place.

Whenever the skull has been absent from the farmhouse, misfortunes have occurred. One farmer who had not taken the superstition seriously found that after scything a swathe through a grass meadow, he turned round to find the grass still upright and uncut. Cattle have died or wandered off, crops have failed, farmworkers have had serious accidents, and the number of disturbances has grown to such an extent that the farmers have recovered the skull from its burial place in order that its curse should be lifted.

Once Dickey was thrown into the nearby Combs Reservoir, but the fish died. Twice it was buried in Chapel-en-le-Frith churchyard, but on both occasions the desperate farmer had to dig it up again. On one occasion it was buried in a manure heap while the house was being rebuilt, but each morning the workmen found that the previous day's work had been undone. They also claimed that their work was being disturbed by the sounds of low groans from the manure. The skull was dug up again and placed on a beam in a barn, and the work was allowed to continue.

Dickey has a kindly side too. Those who treat him with respect find him a benefactor, a guardian spirit even. He has drawn attention to calving cows, warned the farmer of burglars, roused one farmer when a cow was in danger of being accidentally choked by its chain. One tenant, a Mr Bramwell, said that he would rather lose his best animal than be without Dickey's assistance.

When a thief had helped himself to a sackful of potatoes from the garden, he found himself unable to move. The farmer was roused by the sound of rattling pots and pans, and caught the thief. On a separate occasion, a passing waggoner noticed a light in the farmhouse window, and jeered that Dickey was going to bed. His waggon immediately turned over. The man learnt not to mock the skull in the window of Tunstead Farm. Not that Dickey lacked a sense of humour. When a group of young men used the skull as a cup and drank water from it, they suffered no punishment. It was said at the time that Dickey was once young and foolish and had not regarded the prank as an insult.

One of Dickey's greatest victories was over the engineers of the London & North Western Railway Company, who wanted to build a bridge over the road to complete a line across the Combs Valley. This work was to take place on a field belonging to Tunstead Farm, and the farmer objected. Apparently Dickey did too. The railway engineers constructed the bridge, but found that the arches distorted and sank into the ground. They battled on with the problem for many months and at great expense, but in the end they had to admit defeat and move 1/2 mile further away. They recorded the incident as due to quicksands, but the people of the area knew that Dickey had triumphed yet again. This event led the dialect poet, Samuel Laycock, to write:

> 'Neaw, Dickey, be quiet wi' thee, lad
> An' let navvies an' railway be.
> Mon, tha shouldn't do soa, it's too bad,
> What harm are they doin' to thee?
> Deed folk shouldn't meddle at o'
> But leov o' these matters to th'wick.
> They'll see they're done gradely, aw know –
> Dos't y'ear what aw say to thee, Dick?'

DEVON

Something Out of Hell

T he three young men had been to Evensong in a church in the prestigious area of the Warberries in Torquay, South Devon. Little could they have imagined after the calm mood of the service they had just attended, how the next few hours would hold such horror that one of them would later describe it as 'something out of hell'.

The well known novelist and magazine writer Beverley Nichols, his brother and a young friend, Lord St Audries, were spending a few days in this then exclusive watering place favoured by the rich and elderly. It was a warm evening and they decided to wander slowly up Middle Warberry Road admiring the large houses built both sides of the street. Much to their surprise they came upon a derelict house, whose broken gate held the name 'Castel-a-Mare'.

'Come on chaps, let's explore,' Nichols had the natural curiosity of a writer.

The other two, on their way to visit friends, hung back for a moment, but they saw how keen Nichols was, and were now somewhat intrigued themselves by the fearful looking, dilapidated and empty house with its glassless windows. They followed him through the overgrown garden, waist-high in weeds and wild roses, entering the ground floor through a French window consisting only of a rotting wooden frame.

A candle stood in a broken saucer on a shelf. They lighted this and started to walk from room to room – cobwebs hung from the ceilings and the house was damp, smelling of the rotting floorboards which gave way under their feet. Each room was more dank and depressing than the last.

Plaster had dropped from the ceilings in lumps, thick wallpaper hung in strips. The trio were so affected by the atmosphere and an inexplicable aura of evil that they started to drop their voices to a whisper as if they feared disturbing something.

A staircase stretched upwards into the darkness. Nichols had gone ahead and stood waiting for the others to join him. As he did so a curious feeling came over him. He had thought it would simply be creepy as any deserted house might be, but this was something else. The atmosphere had changed as if everything had gone into slow motion, even his sight was blurred as though some dark material had come between him and the outside world. He thought he was going to faint, but feared that if he did some terrible fate would overcome him.

He staggered down the stairs past the other two and outside, sinking thankfully on the damp soft grass and trembling from his experience. A stiff breeze had come up, the evening had turned cool, a window was flapping somewhere on rusted hinges. Getting shakily to his feet, he said he did not want to do any more exploring and suggested to the other two that they went on to meet their friends, but now there was no stopping them.

St Audries ran up the stairs and across the landing to the room where Nichols had been. The other two standing in the garden called after him to keep whistling and they would answer.

Abruptly, St Audries' answering whistle stopped as though someone had put a hand over his mouth.

There was utter silence. Even the breeze had dropped – no sound came from anywhere as if the world itself stood still, holding its breath.

Then a scream came from up the stairs – almost inhuman and yet they could recognise it as St Audries' voice. In his book Nichols said it was a sound 'which I hope I shall never hear again, the kind of cry a man who had been stabbed in the back would make'.

Now came the sound of a terrible struggle, thuds, screams. They ran into the house but St Audries almost knocked them flying in his headlong dash past them, his face ashen, his hair and clothes covered in dust.

At last he managed to speak through tight lips. 'The thing ... it happened, out of the room and down the darkness of the corridor, something raced ... it was black, shaped like a man ...' He paused to gain his breath, leaning on a broken garden seat. 'I just noticed two things – the first was I could see no face, only blackness – the second was it made no noise as it raced at me over the rotting boards ... no sound ... knocking me flat. I had this terrible sensation of evil as though I was struggling with something completely inhuman, something dark, evil.'

When St Audries became more coherent, Nichols discovered it was the same room in which he felt faint. Probably if he had stayed he would have suffered the same fate.

The three men were now thoroughly frightened and out of their depth. They went next door and explained the situation, saying one of them had felt ill. They were given brandy by the householder and its warmth gradually restored them to some kind of normality. From him they learnt the terrible significance of that little room at the top of the stairs ...

Like the Elephant's Child in Kipling's *Just So Stories*, I have an insatiable curiosity and having read Nichols' account of this affair in his book *Twenty-Five* I had to see where Castel-a-Mare had once stood.

In the exact location described by Nichols, opposite a house called Edwinstowe there was a gaping hole like a missing tooth. A high stone wall ran along the road with a white gate in the middle which obviously had once led into the back premises and garden of a house. Next door on one side stood Norfolk Lodge and Grendon, on the other Monte Rosa. There was a big empty patch where once a three storey house had stood.

It was 1979 when I first saw the place. A Mr Reburn was living in Monte Rosa and I called to ask if he could tell me the story of Castel-a-Mare. However, it seems he had not lived there long and had not heard the tale from years ago, but he took me down some cement steps to his garden. This was well below the level of the road as it would have been the cellars of the house.

'I have often wondered why there is only about a foot of earth in my garden and beneath it stones and bricks, obviously from the demolished house, as though a load of earth had been brought to cover them,' he told me. I wondered what else they might cover. He said that he had thought from various tiles and things he had found on his premises that they had once been stables.

'As a matter of fact,' he went on, 'I did wonder from the number of names on the deeds that the house must have changed hands over and over again, but that is really all I know of the history of the place.'

And so I started to research this 'something out of hell', for I must admit that standing among the ruins somehow even the name – 'Castel-a-Mare' – seemed to hold a kind of intangible menace.

To begin at the beginning – it was very difficult from the small amount of information I could glean to decide who actually was the victim and who the assassin in what had obviously been a terrible murder or murders. In one account I read, the house had been owned by a local doctor who had periods of insanity and had murdered his wife and then the little maid who had witnessed the crime, while others said the victim was a guest who had come as a patient to stay with the doctor and whom he murdered. But perhaps after so many years it is not all that important who the victim was or his or her killer – more important is what they left behind.

For years the old house in the Warberries was haunted by the maid who witnessed the brutal murder. This story at least is universal and widespread. She screamed when she saw what was happening, then turned and ran, to be chased from room to room up and down the stairs and along the dark corridors until at last the murderer caught her and strangled her too, the body being put in a cupboard which was later incorporated into a bathroom. This was probably where Nichols and St Audries had their terrible experiences.

And so the ghost of Castel-a-Mare started to haunt the house and, it seems, the stables too, which were so affected that horses could only be forced into them backwards. No doors stayed locked, dogs would not pass the house without whimpering and howling, some owners even had actually to cross the road with them. No tenant would stay, as Mr Reburn had discovered, and eventually the house had fallen into such decay that lead was stolen from the roof, and timber and even bricks were taken. The tales of horror and mystery increased, as did the vandalism.

My fascination with the story increased. I went to talk to a lady by the name of Edna White who was a member of the Devonshire Association and lived in Torquay. She had collected mystery stories of Devon for 20 years and showed me some of the notes she had made from a book written by Violet Tweedale, *Ghosts I Have Seen.*

Violet herself lived in the Warberries and often passed the house. She had heard running footsteps and screams, and listened to gossip about the house and its inmates. Eventually she found out the man who owned it – a builder – and asked if she might make some investigations. He gave his consent.

This was the story Edna told me. The house was demolished in 1920 as a result of all the damage, but before that happened, in 1913, Violet and her husband made the first investigation. It produced very little except a feeling of intense cold and a chilling sensation as if they were being watched, she remarked, 'by something intensely evil'.

In 1917 Violet was asked to join a party of people who intended to investigate the house with the aid of a medium. This had come about through a soldier who was home on leave and was interested and very knowledgeable in psychic research – he had organised the party and invited several people including Violet.

The medium chose a bedroom on the first floor next to the bathroom. After some little time she suddenly started to give vent to a volley of violent language in the deep-toned voice of a man, asking what right all these intruders had to be in his house. There was a rather unpleasant scene, for although the medium was a comparatively elderly lady – and frail – suddenly she was controlled by this 'man' of superhuman strength who bellowed out terrible language, without warning attacking the soldier and throwing him to the ground. Two others in the party had to go to his aid, but with herculean strength the medium threw them all back against the wall, forcing them to the top of the stairs, obviously with the intention of throwing them down. There was a scuffle during which the onlookers were helpless. Any moment it seemed someone would be seriously injured.

Then as suddenly as the poor woman had been possessed, it all ended. The medium crashed to the floor, the onlookers fearing she must be dead. Quickly they picked her up and took her out into the fresh air where gradually she recovered. Someone had a brandy flask and this revived her. And then to everyone's amazement, the soldier asked her if she felt inclined to repeat the experiment a few days later.

The others protested that it would be cruel, asking for trouble, but she agreed. It might risk her life, they said, but she was adamant.

So a week later they all gathered once more in the house. One or two other people had heard of the last event and joined the original party. This time the soldier assured them he was prepared – he did seem to have considerable experience in this kind of happening and stated he intended to exorcise the 'entity' as he described it – whoever or whatever 'it' might be.

This led to an almost incredible encounter in which, as in a boxing ring, the fight swayed back and forth between one protagonist and another.

At first it seemed the soldier would overcome the medium and she started to cry as if she had changed into a heartbroken young girl. She babbled incoherently between sobs that shook her – 'Poor master … there on the bed … help him, help him, help him …' over and over again – then clenched her hands to her throat as if she were trying to tear away other hands that were strangling her. Was this the culmination of some horrifying murder that had occurred on that very spot?

Suddenly the air was rent by the most piercing, bloodcurdling screams as the medium now turned as if she were an animal at bay, struggling with something unseen, wrestling wildly, fighting for her very own life while all the time the terrible screams came from her.

In vain the others tried to help her, to drag her away from this invisible murderer, but it was impossible to seize an intangible, disembodied spirit.

At last two of the onlookers managed to get her against the wall and stood in front so they could try to defend her against the original spirit which had controlled her. The poor woman was gasping for breath, trying to speak in a young girl's voice, hoarse with emotion.

'He'll kill me next! He's killed the master! Someone help!'

At last the power of the soldier's exorcism apparently triumphed – if that was indeed what it was. He managed to control the medium and discover from the spirit that possessed her that the man had been insane when the murder took place and she was the little maid who shared the victim's fate – but whether the victim was the doctor of the patient did not become clear.

Violet Tweedale tracked down the records which verified the names and dates of the various residents of the village but by then, of course, these violent events had all taken place at least 50 years before and there was no one alive who could confirm the actual story.

If it is true, and I have no reason to doubt it, it does have to fall into the category of the perfect murder, for no record of any killing is recorded in those times by anyone who was then alive.

In her book Mrs Tweedale added something which interested me very much and was to come to mind years later. She said, 'I do not know if it is intended to build another house on the same site, I hope not for it is very probable even a new residence would share the fate of the old – bricks and mortar are no impediment to the disembodied and there is no reason why they should not elect to manifest within an indefinite period of time.'

Her account is dated 1920 which would make the date of the murder sometime in about 1870.

Edna White told me she had tried to trace the owners and tenants of the property but up to now all she had found was a Mrs Dove in 1857 and a Mr Benjamin Fulwood in 1878/9. It was owned by a builder whose name she thought was E.P. Bovey and he lived opposite in Edwinstowe.

When I asked her what she thought of the whole affair she added one explanation for there being no recording of the murder: if it was the patient who died, the male victim, said to be a foreigner, could have been given a death certificate by the doctor who murdered him and thus a normal burial. But what about the little maid, what happened to her body?

A couple of summers ago I went back to see what had happened, if anything, to the shades of Castel-a-Mare. A huge new house was being built. I talked to the builders who were having a tea break.

'Anything odd happened here at all? I asked. For a moment they just grinned at me, 'another barmy old bird' I expect they thought. Then one put down his mug.

'Well, we did think some vandals had been in and moved our ladders and upset tins of paint. We'd locked them all up and no one had actually broken in – it's the new bathroom top of the stairs – made us feel a bit spooky.'

I decided not to tell them about the 'something out of hell'. They might be tempted to pass it on to the new owner and as my old Devonshire granny used to say, 'What you don't know can't hurt you.'

Not too sure in this case.

The Ghostly Highway

An article in the *Sunday Express* in April 1979 described how a Mrs Davidson was driving home in the winter moonlight on a well known road near her home when suddenly the way ahead was no longer familiar – part of it blacked out, a road she had never seen before forked mistily away to her right. It seems nine people had died on that piece of carriageway in Kent since November 1977.

This brought vividly to mind the most famous of all mysteries to do with highways in Devon – that of the Hairy Hands.

Many roads in Devon are haunted by phantoms either visible or audible to many people. Usually there is a pervading aura of something tragic or evil which some say accounts for otherwise inexplicable accidents. Obviously, of all these, those on Dartmoor roads must come top of the list. The atmosphere anyway is eerie, and it is easy enough to become disorientated in the low mist which often occurs. And there have been many unexplained incidents where the traveller sees or feels a huge pair of hairy hands interfering with handlebars or steering wheel.

So is there some kind of reserve of psychic power in the area? Is it simply a manifestation of force? In this case there does not seem to be any mention of it before the second decade of the 20th century. Perhaps it is the presence of some malignant influence or matter which once created can never be destroyed – neither of the human nor of the spirit world but earthbound between the two, freed from the body but not from the scene of some crime committed during life on this earth.

Perhaps violent death and emotions can leave imprints on the ether, concentrated with such force as to form definite emanations. Is this more far fetched than imagining what effect it would have had on a prehistoric man if he had seen a personality on a television screen, appearing out of a box, which is something we take as perfectly normal today.

These particular happenings occur between Postbridge and Two Bridges in the Ancherton region of the Moor. Only once was I frightened in this spot, when I got enveloped in a typical Dartmoor mist, thick and obliterating so that I suddenly felt a complete isolation in time and place. Perhaps it was the utter silence after the constant racket we live in today, but there is a very narrow margin between loneliness and plain fear. I only know that now I avoid that place on my own.

This area became of interest to the general public in the early 1920s. In 1921 there were three motoring accidents near the gate of Archerton Drive on Nine Mile Hill, reported in the *Daily Mail* on 14th and 15th October. The first had been in March when Dr Helby, the prison doctor from Princetown, had been asked to attend an inquest at Postbridge. He was riding a bike with a sidecar containing two children, daughters of the Deputy Governor of the prison, and his own wife, Mrs Helby. Suddenly the machine swerved, the engine literally detaching itself as he was flung into the ditch and his neck broken. The children and his wife fell on the verge and were not seriously hurt but naturally terrified.

Having written an account of this, I had a letter from a Dr Adkin of Exmouth. He told me that when he was a small boy he and his family were staying on holiday at Cherrybrook Farm near to Archerton not far from where the old powder mill and buildings still stand, and recalled this incident well.

They were passing a small gravel pit dug out by the road men to repair potholes before the days of tarmac – the family were on their way to their holiday cottage on the farm. There were signs of an accident a little way ahead and his father, a doctor, telling his family to stay where they were, went to see if he could help.

He realised immediately that the man was dead. He managed to get some words out of the wife, who said that as they approached the place where the accident occurred her husband had cried out that he had lost control of the machine and something about 'hair' and 'hands' which made no sense.

The Ghostly Highway between Postbridge and Two Bridges

A few weeks later a motor coach mounted the bank on the Lake side of the road and one woman was badly hurt. The driver said, 'I felt hands pull the wheel towards the Lake side', but no one listened to him.

Later that year, on a dull, foggy Friday – 26th August – an Army officer was riding a motor bike and was again thrown on the verge in exactly the same place. He only suffered shock and scratches but he was a very experienced rider. He said, 'It was just not my fault, something seemed to wrench me off the road, a huge hairy pair of hands closed over mine on the handlebars. I tried to fight them but they were too strong.'

As all these stories gradually gained prominence, the *Daily Mail* sent investigators to the spot and their report appeared that October. Eventually the camber of the road was altered, but it made no difference and in any case all these vehicles had turned over upwards to the Lake side, both the coach and the officer's cycle travelling uphill.

Forty years later, in 1961, a young man was driving from Plymouth to

Chagford when his car overturned on exactly the same spot. He was found dead underneath it. In spite of a thorough examination of the body by forensic experts, and of the mechanism of the car, no explanation of the accident could be given.

In 1991 a doctor from Somerset turned his car over at the same place. He said, like the others, it was as if some malignant force had sent it out of control. The atmosphere inside the car was deathly cold, literally paralysing him. He shook all over and again said, 'It was as if something evil was actually inside the car with me, the steering wheel went wild and was wrenched out of my hands.'

Someone else who knew much about this drama was Theo Brown, that expert on all to do with folklore, mystery and ghosts in Devon. She told me what a Mrs Battiscombe had described to her; she was the widow of the successor to the prison doctor from Princetown who had been killed.

'A young man who was a guest at Penlee in Postbridge undertook to run in to Princetown on his motorbike to get something for his hostess,' she said. 'In about an hour he returned to Penlee very white and shaken saying he had had a most frightening experience. He had felt his hands gripped by two rough and hairy hands which made every effort to throw him off his machine. He never got much beyond the clapper bridge.'

Theo's own parents knew the area very well, for a month each summer they used to park a caravan among the old ruins of the powder mill a mile west of Postbridge, half a mile north of the haunted road.

One night when the family were asleep in their bunks in the caravan Theo had woken up with a premonition of danger. Suddenly she was wide awake and looking up at the little window above her bunk she saw fingers and the palm of a very large hand with hairs on it – it was clawing at the top of the window which was a little way open.

'I had the feeling that the owner of the hand was about to harm us – it was no human hand.' She made the sign of the cross and prayed to God to keep them from harm. Slowly the hand sank down the window out of sight. They stayed on for the rest of the holiday but she never felt any evil near the caravan again.

One curious fact about these hauntings is that four of the people affected in accidents were doctors, including Dr Helby, Dr Adkin senior who helped at the accident, and his son, Dr Adkin, who had written to me although only a child at the time. The latter did not mention in his letter whether he had ever driven along this piece of road since. Perhaps he had felt discretion was the better part of valour! Number four was the doctor from Somerset whose name we do not know. Possibly this spirit, ghost or whatever, had a special grudge against the medical profession for some reason.

As I write, it is some years since there have been any reports of 'happenings' here but, as I said before, it is not a place I would walk alone.

DORSET

The Durweston Poltergeist

P sychic disturbance and teenage girls seem on occasion to be linked, and this may in some way explain the strange happenings at Durweston during the winter of 1894-95. The case, which involved two orphan girls, attracted great national attention at the time and subsequently, and was mentioned in various learned journals and books, including Dr Paul Joire's *Psychical and Supernormal Phenomena*. This is the story ...

Durweston is a tiny hamlet not far from Blandford Forum, and on the opposite bank of the Stour from Stourpaine. At Norton, an isolated spot some way from the main village, stood two houses some distance from the road, and on the edge of a wood. The houses were attached, and in one lived a Mrs Best. To this house came two children, girls aged four and thirteen – orphans from a workhouse who had been boarded out in order to give them a change from their sad surroundings through the philanthropy of two sisters, the Misses Pitt of Iwerne Steepleton. Mrs Best was a respectable woman, well liked in the small community. It seemed an ideal situation.

Soon after the girls arrived at Norton odd happenings began to trouble the house, scratchings and knockings – faint at first, but growing in volume as time went on – were heard, and no apparent source was found. In the end they became so loud as to be described by a member of the Society for Psychical Research as 'like hammer blows'. Then these were replaced by even more startling phenomena – stones and other objects began to fly about, apparently for no reason, and things came hurtling through windows but without breaking them, before returning the way they came.

Odd happenings at Durweston

The place was thoroughly searched by several interested groups and individuals; the rector, the local schoolmaster, spiritualists – even the Duke of Argyll – came to Durweston to examine first-hand the strange happenings.

From here the girls were moved down the road to another cottage in the village, the home of a Mr Cross. They took the phenomena with them; loud bangs were heard, plaster fell from the walls and ceilings and again, objects flew around unaided.

By now the local press became involved, and a flood of letters with suggested explanations were published. Many people of course considered the whole thing a fraud, but others, including the local vicar, the Rev W.M. Anderson, believed that what had occurred was an authentic psychic event of some importance.

It was recalled that a similar incident had happened in the home of the

Rev Samuel Wesley, father of the famous John Wesley, founder of the Methodist Church. During 1716 his home at Epworth in Lincolnshire was haunted by a poltergeist for about two months; Wesley considered it a Devil-spirit. Here too, it was linked to the presence of a girl, young Hetty Wesley. It would cause a loud knocking on the headboard of her bed. The old man would roar: 'Thou deaf and dumb devil, why dost thou frighten these children?' In fact Hetty, also in her early teens, and her young toddler sister were not at all frightened. They called the poltergeist 'Old Jeffrey' and would chase it round the house!

At Durweston no such pursuit is recorded. The mystery was never solved and peace did not return to the village until the two orphans left. They first went to Iwerne Minster, where the strange happenings continued, and then after that, to London where it was reported not long after that the eldest girl had died.

So it would seem that the manifestation came from the children themselves. Yet there is one footnote which may or may not be related to this strange tale. There is a local legend in Durweston which tells of a ghost which once walked in the part of the parish where the Rectory garden now stands. The story goes that the figure took the form of a nurse, and if she was seen by a child, the child was said to die within a year. The Bishop was called, Holy water was sprinkled and apparently the ghost was laid. And perhaps it was, for there were no further reports of psychic phenomena after the departure of the two girls. Yet the two stories seem to have a tantalising connection, and like all the best ghost stories are destined to remain a mystery!

❖

The Rider of Bottlebrush Down

England has many apparitions from the past who sometimes return across the centuries to visit our own time, but Dorset surely beats them all with its Bronze Age horseman.

Archaeologist Dr Richard C.C. Clay had been with a team excavating a Bronze Age settlement at Pokesdown, Dorset in 1924 and at the end of the day was on his way back to Salisbury. As he describes it in his own account: 'I was motoring home along the straight road which cuts the open downland between Cranborne and Sixpenny Handley and had reached the spot between the small clump of beech trees to the east and Squirrels Corner pinewood to the west, where the road dips before rising to cross the Roman road from Badbury Rings to Old Sarum.'

Suddenly he noticed a figure on horseback, riding over the fields and going in the same direction as himself, who turned and galloped as if to reach the road ahead of him. Dr Clay instinctively slowed down, thinking that the rider would cross ahead of his car. But instead he turned, and began to gallop parallel to the road, about 50 yards away.

Dr Clay had a good view of his companion, and was amazed at what he saw. As he said afterwards, 'I could see he was no ordinary horseman, for he had bare legs and wore a long, loose coat. His horse had a long mane and tail, but I could see neither bridle nor stirrup. His face was turned towards me, but I was unable to see his features. He seemed to be threatening me with some implement, which he waved above his head in his right hand.'

Dr Clay realised that what he was seeing was a prehistoric man; then even as he watched, horse and rider simply vanished. He carefully noted the spot, and next day when he returned to the place he found that it coincided with a low, round barrow close to the road, something he could not remember ever noticing before.

He was hopeful that next time he drove along the same road he might have another sighting of the horse and rider, but although he passed that way in the evening for several weeks afterwards they never reappeared. But he had a clear recollection of the horseman, and he was certain that what he had seen was an apparition from the late Bronze Age, the period between 700 and 600 BC.

Although Dr Clay never saw the rider of Bottlebrush Down again, his was not the only sighting. In the B3081 area which runs between Cranborne and Sixpenny Handley, farmers and shepherds have seen him galloping across the fields, and a year or two after the doctor's strange experience a friend wrote to tell him that two girl cyclists had quite a fright one night as they pedalled along towards Cranborne when the ghostly horseman suddenly appeared, and rode along beside them before just as suddenly disappearing!

He also heard of a young couple in 1945 who were sitting on the grass in the same area when they heard the sound of galloping hooves very close. Instinctively they both crouched down with their hands over their heads and felt a rush of cold air as the sound went past them at terrific speed.

There is a story too of an old shepherd who used to have a flock of sheep on Handley Downs. Every day he would sit there eating his dinner, and afterwards he always smoked his pipe. One day he was resting on a bank by Squirrels Corner, and as he filled his pipe he noticed a man on horseback come out of the green lane between the trees on his right. At that moment he realised to his annoyance that he had forgotten his matches, so he got up and walked towards the horseman, intending to ask him for a light. But just as he approached, both horse and rider vanished!

❖

The Skull That Screamed

I n the realms of British folklore, screaming skull stories must rank among the most strange and horrifying. The legend in every case is much the same. The skull must never be moved from its home or the consequences will be dire. Invariably when such attempts have been made, all kinds of disasters have ensued and life has been made impossible for the family, with horrendous screaming heard, only ceasing on the restoration of the skull to its former residence.

Bettiscombe is a beautiful old manor house not far from Lyme Regis in Dorset, famous for its own screaming skull. The house was the home of the Pinney family for many years but the story really starts in 1685 when Azariah Pinney, the local squire, took part in the ill-fated Monmouth rebellion, and was subsequently exiled to the West Indian island of Nevis. But he prospered there, and eventually his grandson, John Pinney, was able to return to his family's roots, bringing with him a faithful negro servant. But although the man settled happily in his new home, his health deteriorated and his master promised him that when he died his body would be taken back to Nevis. However, John Pinney died first, and when his negro servant died soon afterwards, he was buried in the churchyard near his master.

The consequences were horrendous. The farmhouse was in an uproar as doors and windows banged, shaking the building, and weird screaming from the churchyard alarmed the village. Crops failed and animals died, until the skull was removed from the graveyard and brought back to the house and kept in an attic room.

But that was not the end of the skull's adventures. It is said that at the beginning of the 20th century a tenant had leased Bettiscombe and during a Christmas party, full of festive sprit he lightheartedly threw the skull into a horse pond near the house. One can imagine the general consternation when next morning the skull was found on the doorstep. To get there it would have had to cross a patio and climb a flight of steps! And what of the tradition that anyone responsible for interfering with the skull would die within a year? Apparently sometime in the Thirties, a young Australian called at Bettiscombe and explained that he was the son of the former tenant, who, after emigrating to Australia, had died suddenly within a year of the horse pond incident.

Another story has it that the skull belonged to a young girl who was kept prisoner in an attic room at the manor, and who may have been murdered. Certainly when the skull was examined in the Fifties at the Royal College of Surgeons, it was thought that it was that of a young

John Frederick Pinney and Bettiscombe's screaming skull

female with delicate features, much more ancient than had been thought, and possibly even of prehistoric origin.

Behind Bettiscombe manor house rise the slopes of Pilsdon Pen, a prehistoric settlement with burial mounds, and it seems quite possible that the skull may have originally come from there, en route for its eventual resting place at Bettiscombe, where it still remains.

DURHAM

The Ghosts of Raby Castle

R aby Castle, once one of the strongholds of the powerful Neville family, is still haunted by Charles Neville, Earl of Westmorland who was forced to surrender it to Henry VIII after the unsuccessful Rising of the Northern Earls. His apparition has been seen en route for the Baron's Hall where in 1569 he and his men were deciding that such a venture would be unwise when they were interrupted by his feisty wife who upbraided them as cowards. Stung by her words they fought, and lost. And the Earl fled to Scotland, and then to Holland where he is buried, but his ghost still returns to haunt his former home.

The castle passed to the Vane family, one of whom, Henry Vane the Younger, was imprisoned there by the Stuarts and ordered to be executed. His attempt to make a last speech to his people was drowned out on the orders of the Sherriff who instructed trumpeters to blow loudly

The much haunted Raby Castle

so that he could not be heard. Undaunted, Henry was still speaking as his head rolled off!

His headless ghost is seen sitting in the library at Raby, his head on the desk before him, the lips moving as if he is still making that unfinished speech.

The Barnard family followed at Raby, and the first Lady Barnard was known for her fearsome temper, caused apparently because she disapproved of her son's choice of bride. She still haunts the battlements, eyes glowing with fury as she knits with red hot needles! She is known locally as Old Hell Cat!

To round off the area's quota of ghosts, the murdered victims of Maria Cotton, hung for her crimes in Durham in 1873, merrily chase each other in a macabre game of follow-my-leader through the countryside surrounding Raby's much haunted castle.

The Grey Lady of Crossgate Peth

P hantom hitchhikers seem a modern phenomenon since most accounts feature a motorist who picks up a roadside traveller who later mysteriously disappears en route without opening the car door. But Durham has its own 14th century ghost, a sad and silent Grey Lady, her new baby in her arms, who frequented Crossgate Peth in time gone by in search of a lift. The drivers of coaches and wagons often drew up in the area for a rest and refreshment, and many of them noticed that there was sometimes a sudden, inexplicable drop in temperature.

Then as their journey continued they noticed that they were carrying a mysterious passenger, a quiet young woman with a small baby. She remained with them until they reached Neville's Cross where she would just as suddenly disappear.

This was the site of the Battle of Neville's Cross in 1346 between the armies of the English and the Scots, and it is believed that the girl's husband was one of the soldiers who lost their lives there and the reason for her sorrow was because she had begged him not to enlist, and when he did she had refused to bid him a loving farewell. Now she was journeying to the battlefield in the hope of finding his body.

Sightings of the sorrowing Grey Lady have been scarce in modern times as she seems to have disappeared with the horse-drawn carriages and carts of earlier times. Did she find the beloved husband she sought? Who knows? Perhaps one day a modern driver may draw up for a hitchhiker and find that his passenger is a sad and silent Grey Lady from the 14th century.

ESSEX

The Farm in the Marshes

R elaxing in the comfortable sitting room with a friendly cat on my lap I had no uneasy feelings. And yet I had come to this isolated farm on the Essex marshes to hear first hand about a succession of paranormal happenings here that had at first aroused curiosity in its new occupants but later caused alarm and apprehension. Because everything happened so recently, I have changed the names of those involved in order to preserve their anonymity.

Chris and her husband David moved into the farm with their two year old daughter, Lynn, in the late summer of 1989. 'We've never been tuned into ghosts or been interested in that sort of thing,' Chris told me. 'When we came to live here it was the last thing on our minds, we were so busy getting settled in.' There was a lot to do putting the rather neglected house in order and from time to time when they noticed footsteps outside they assumed it was just someone passing by in the lane. But about three weeks after they arrived, Chris awoke in the night to hear the sound of someone walking about right underneath the bedroom window.

'They were very heavy footsteps,' she explained, 'like someone wearing wellingtons, and gave the impression of someone very tall taking long strides.'

David heard them too, and went down to check outside while Chris looked down from the window, but although the heavy tramp of someone walking around close by could still be heard, there was no one to see.

'We found out later talking to neighbours that an old ploughman used to live here, and he was in the habit of walking round the farm at night checking on his livestock,' said Chris. 'And', she went on, 'we think he's still here. Apparently he was a very big man, 6 foot 4 inches tall, and the footsteps we heard certainly sounded like someone with a long stride.

They continued to hear the disembodied footsteps from time to time, but took little notice as now there were the sounds of the farm animals and their four dogs which helped to mask other noises. However, their little girl had started talking to an invisible new friend whom she called John. When asked, she would say he was a nice man, and she chatted away as she sat at her little desk drawing a picture for John. Chris noticed that as she talked, Lynn was looking high up towards the ceiling as if John was up there – or, or course, as if he was very tall!

'We asked her what John looked like', said Chris, 'and she described a man who sounded just like the old ploughman. Neighbours who had known him said what a nice person he was, very much a gentleman. He sounded like someone you would have liked to know, and I feel sure he was not the cause of our problems here.'

As Chris and David started to restock the farm, they let out the stables to various people for their horses, but no one seemed to stay long. 'People said they felt there were often voices calling them by name. They thought it was us, but it wasn't. Some said they were conscious of an uneasy atmosphere they didn't like, and this seemed to be gradually building up.

'I was working in the dairy late one night when I heard my husband call me. I answered, and went out and met him outside as he thought I had called him. We then both distinctly heard a woman's voice call David by name. It seemed to be coming from the pig pens but when we looked round there was no one there, and the animals seemed undisturbed.'

Another strange happening that Chris described is the sound of a car arriving and driving up to the barn. The engine stops and then there is the sound of a car door opening and a woman's voice calls 'COO-ee'.

'It sounds so normal', Chris told me, 'that time and time again I have gone to look but there is no car, and no one there. It is so real that you just accept it is someone arriving.

'I have been told that during the last war women from the WVS used to deliver things to the men on the gun sites here, and once a car drove into the wall outside and crashed. It was a fatal accident and we wondered if this could have something to do with the sounds we hear. It's odd because it sounds as if the car is drawing up on gravel. There isn't any gravel now, and hasn't been for ages, but there was gravel in the yard during the war and early 1950s.'

After about a year, the family started noticing cold feelings throughout the house, and Chris told of an odd sensation of pressure building up that was difficult to describe. Then sometimes when she was working in the kitchen she would notice, out of the corner of her eye, something moving.

'I'd brush back my hair, thinking it was nothing more than that,' she said, 'but it was like a shadow dancing across the hall. Once I was sitting reading and looked up to see a shadow pass along the wall. It was like smoke. And on another occasion I saw a ball shape pass along the bottom of the wall. My husband often complained because I left the lights on all over the house, but a feeling of uneasiness was making me jumpy.

'One Christmas I was in the kitchen cooking while my husband went to have a drink with some neighbours. I had the radio on playing carols while I was working, and hadn't noticed how dark it was getting, but suddenly for no reason an awful feeling of depression came over me. I'd never felt anything like it before, I just wanted to curl up and shut everything out. I hadn't been thinking about anything ghostly at all, but now I was becoming really tense and frightened. When my husband came back he switched the lights on and found me hunched up in a corner in the dark.

'After Christmas, I was sitting on the floor by the fire one night and David was outside in the barn. I heard footsteps outside and then the side door opened. I assumed it was David but he didn't come into the room. When he did arrive later I told him what had happened and we thought there might have been an intruder as the sounds had been so real. So we checked the house, but there was no one around.'

As time went on the atmosphere in the house didn't improve. A neighbour who visited them for dinner one night said he thought he saw something like a shadow passing across the hall which made him feel nervous. There was a cold spot in the office which several people noticed. And little Lynn said she saw books and other things move of their own accord, and once she saw a pair of shoes 'walk down the hall'.

'We decided to put the farm up for sale,' said Chris, 'we really didn't want to stay any longer. It seemed an unlucky place, apart from the strange happenings. We were having business problems and we'd lost four healthy young dogs one after the other. But although several people came to look over the farm, we didn't manage to sell it.'

But something had to be done and, feeling that the happenings at the farm were something outside their experience, Chris and David asked their local Roman Catholic minister to visit them.

His first words were 'I sense that you need more than a blessing.' He walked from room to room in the house, saying 'If you come in peace, stay, but if not, be gone', and then said prayers in each room and blessed it. Afterwards he said prayers over each of the family, and blessed them too. He had brought a large crucifix with him and left it with them as a protection and, in fact, they now have a crucifix in every room of the house.

'After he had finished I was amazed at the difference,' said Chris. 'The whole house felt warmer, the atmosphere was lighter, and everyone was happier. It was a pleasure to come home. And when the next fuel bill came it was less than a third of the previous one.'

So is the haunting at an end? Not exactly. Chris told me that if they talk about it to anyone, something always happens. They were out with some friends recently, and an elderly neighbour was babysitting. When they got home she told them that about an hour before there had been a curious scratching noise in the chimney as if a large bird was scrabbling away with its claws. And when they thought about it they realised that it must have been about that time that they were telling their friends about the strange goings on at the farm.

And only a few days before my visit, Chris was discussing the happenings at the farm with someone else and when she arrived home she found that three drinking glasses had been stacked inside each other in the kitchen and the middle one was completely shattered leaving the other two undamaged. What is disturbing the peace of this isolated farm? The old ploughman's footsteps and the sound of the car that never arrives seem simply like echoes of the recent past. But what of the rest?

The farm is set in a lonely area of creeks, rivers and marshland on the edge of the estuary, a part of Essex with a remarkable heritage of strange stories of ancient ghosts, witches and smugglers, not forgetting the spectral black hound of Odin. Even the Prince of Darkness himself apparently figured prominently in the lives of Essex inhabitants centuries ago. Many places still bear his name, like Devil's Wood, Devil's Walls, Devil's Steps and the Devil's Field, and one often told legend is sited close by the haunted farmhouse I visited that day.

It seems that a medieval knight planned to build a house in Devil's Wood but, after a moat had been dug and building started, every night the day's work was demolished. So the knight and his two dogs kept guard one night to catch the culprit, and to his consternation it was the Devil who arrived with his hounds. It's said that the Devil was furious that the knight had chosen to build his house in this wood as it was where he held his revels.

He then picked up a beam and threw it to the top of a nearby hill with the words 'Where this beam doth fall, there build Barn Hall'.

Barn Hall was duly built at Tolleshunt Knights and the 'Devil's Beam' can still be seen in the cellar, with marks on it described as the Devil's clawmarks.

Alas for the knight who had originally chosen such an unfortunate building site; the Devil swore that when he died he would have his soul, whether he was buried inside or outside the church. To thwart the Devil, the knight was eventually interred half in and half out of the wall of the church at Tolleshunt Knights, where some say the scratches on the tomb are due to the Devil's frantic and unsuccessful attempts to reach the knight inside.

Curiously enough, a field nearby known as Moat Field is believed to be the very place where the knight originally intended to build his house. This field has long had a reputation for being haunted, but a young man's experience there around 1980 suggests that local people who give the place a wide berth have good reason.

At the time of this happening the farmer who owned it asked his son to get the field ploughed as soon as they had finished the harvest. It was quite late in the day before the young man was able to start ploughing and he was still at work that evening when dusk had started to fall.

He switched on the tractor's powerful lights and continued his work although the rest of the field was now in darkness. Then suddenly he was attracted by a movement out of the corner of his eye, but when he turned his head there seemed to be nothing and he thought he must have glimpsed a passing bird or animal. But almost immediately the flicker of another shadow caught his eye, and then another and another, just momentary sightings as if whatever it was was trying to keep out of view. The young man was becoming alarmed as, turning round, he thought he could see other shadowy forms behind his tractor, and as he twisted this way and that trying to peer through the darkness beyond his tractor's beam, his foot slipped off the pedal, causing the engine to stall, and the tractor lurched to a stop.

Becoming more and more agitated he tried repeatedly to restart his tractor, aware that he seemed to be surrounded by moving shadows. And then, to his horror, he heard a click and saw the door handle begin to move. In a panic he turned the ignition key again, and this time the engine started and he began to drive at full speed across the newly ploughed furrows, bouncing crazily towards the gate, conscious that as the lights illuminated the surrounding field there were shadowy forms just on the edge of his vision. And as he passed the moat and its surrounding woodland the tractor lurched sideways and the lights went out.

Thankful that he had almost reached the gate he suddenly heard the sound of the door handle being rattled. He grabbed it and pushed the lock button as a hefty blow on the side of the tractor shook his cab, then at full throttle, he rocketed through the gate and out onto the road and home as fast as he could go.

In the safety of the yard at home he examined the outside of his tractor, and found the right side badly dented and long, deep scratches all round the door handle. After the lad's terrifying experience the farmer sold the field as soon as he could, but that nightmare evening had a lasting effect on his son, who still avoids night ploughing, in fact he is not keen on even driving his car after dark.

So what is the mystery of Moat Field and why do local people say it is haunted? Memories are long in the countryside and folklore often has a basis in fact. In her *Ghosthunter's Guide to Essex* Jessie Payne suggests that the old story of the Devil objecting to the first proposed site of Barn Hall could possibly have had something to do with Devil worshipping rites in pagan times in what is now called Devil's Wood. And those dark menacing shadows in Moat Field that night, what were they?

Essex is a strange county, haunted by the spirits of Romans, Vikings, Crusaders, witches and long dead queens, and more ordinary people like you and me. There are many unexplained mysteries in its lonely places, some almost as isolated as they were centuries ago, and who knows what lurks in the darkness, just out of sight?

GLOUCESTERSHIRE

Gloucestershire Ghosts

In an area like the wolds of Gloucestershire which, until a comparatively short time ago, was bleak, wild and rugged, with thickly forested areas and few roads, it isn't surprising that the county abounds with ghosts, apparitions, spectres, headless horsemen, black hounds, and strange noises in the night!

Take for example the Mickleton Hooter! Mickleton is a north Gloucestershire fringe village; a lively place with a thriving sense of community, and few creepy spots. Except, of course, for Weeping Hollow where the Mickleton Hooter is to be heard in the still of a moonlight night.

Another name for the creature is 'Belhowja' and the earliest explanation concerns Sir Edward Greville, who owned vast areas of land in Gloucestershire in the 16th century. A wealthy man, and a doting parent, for he had but one son to inherit all his acres. All Sir Edward's hopes were pinned upon his one surviving son, but legend has it that Sir Edward shot the boy dead one night in Weeping Hollow in mistake for a robber, and it is the boy's ghost that makes the fearful sounds the locals call the Mickleton Hooter. The place is called Weeping Hollow because of Sir Edward's terrible grief and remorse. The distraught man sold all his lands in 1597 and left the place forever.

Not very far off, near Dover's Hill, scene of the famous Cotswold Olympic Games, poor Beatrice walks on the first evening after the moon is full, clad in a white silk cloak. At one time there was a gate on this very spot known as 'White Lady's Gate' but this name has now largely been forgotten. The story goes that Beatrice and her brothers, John and Maurice, were Puritans who espoused the Parliamentarian cause during the English Civil War. Their near neighbour, Sir Roger, fought on the Royalist side, and when Charles I was beheaded and Cromwell and the Commonwealth ruled our land, Sir Roger took to highway robbery to earn a living because he had been forced to forfeit all his lands and possessions. He earned for himself the nickname of 'The Black Knight'.

His 'beat' was the road to Broadway, and one memorable day he waylaid the coach in which Beatrice was travelling. She recognised his voice, for she had known him from childhood. Inevitably they fell in love, and arranged their trysts at the foot of Dover's Hill. Knowing that her brothers would be both angry and violent Beatrice kept their trysts a secret, and would let Sir Roger know when the coast was clear by waving her white silk cloak as a signal. Her brothers, however, mindful of the need to protect their younger sister, discovered the secret and poor Beatrice was sent away to stay with relatives while they lay in wait for the hapless Sir Roger.

They set an ambush for him, using Beatrice's white silk cloak. Up rode Sir Roger expecting to see his beloved, only to be instantly set upon by John and Maurice and slain. Upon hearing that her lover was killed, poor Beatrice lost her reason, and was confined in a madhouse. She was allowed by a kindly attendant to wear her white silk cloak on the first evening after the full moon. Some say she still does, and flits silently and mournfully around the foot of Dover's Hill, a small sad wraith, still waiting for her lover, the gallant Sir Roger.

Prestbury, near Cheltenham, is said to be one of the most haunted villages in Gloucestershire, although it is less of a village now than of yore. Its proximity to Cheltenham and its busy road have altered its character, but not apparently, quite got rid of all its spectres.

One most romantic ghost is the Cavalier and his horse. During the Civil War, the inhabitants of Prestbury were Parliamentarian to a man. In order to help their cause, and probably to afford themselves some protection, they operated a kind of road block in the form of a rope stretched across the main road through the village.

One dark night, the sound of a galloping horse was heard, and the rope successfully dismounted a Royalist despatch rider. This unfortunate soldier was given no quarter, but was executed on the spot.

He it is who gallops furiously through the village on dark moonless nights.

A strange tale is told of Snowshill Manor, a village of the northern hills of Gloucestershire, and once the home of the wealthy and eccentric Charles Wade. It is now a National Trust property. It remains as Mr Wade left it, and as he himself arranged it.

When Charles Wade began restoring the rooms on the first floor of the house, some visitors said they 'felt something'. There was obviously a mystery here. Charles Wade sent a fragment of the roof timber to a lady clairvoyant of excellent repute, without telling her where it came from. She wrote back to him that she felt two houses on a steep slope, the larger lofty and mysterious. In the upper room, late at night, a girl in a green dress of the 17th century, greatly agitated, paces up and down the room. She doesn't live here and will not stay.

Charles Wade later discovered the story behind the clairvoyant's impressions. In this room Ann Parsons, a sixteen year old heiress, had been secretly married against her will to Anthony Palmer, who wanted her fortune. It was the eve of St Valentine, 1604, and it was midnight. Mr Stone, Vicar of Snowshill, performed the ceremony, 'contrary to the laws of God and the Church', and the affair ended up in the proceedings of the Star Chamber.

Ann was desperately unhappy at being forcibly wed for her money. She refused to spend the wedding night at Snowshill, so the wedding party had to set off on that dark, cold night to pass the night in an hostelry.

Mr Wade named the room at Snowshill Manor 'Ann's Room'.

At Sheepscombe, one of the loveliest spots in the whole of Gloucestershire, a valley of beech clad slopes and ancient woodland, there once stood a hunting lodge. At first a fairly simple building, but later on greatly enlarged and refurbished. It was here that Anne Boleyn and Henry VIII visited Sir William Kingston, and stayed to enjoy hunting in the Cotswolds.

Later, when Sir William was Governor of the Tower of London, he had charge of Anne Boleyn as she awaited her execution. Anne is said to wander still in Sheepscombe Woods, sometimes accompanied by a happy and smiling Henry VIII, both dressed for hunting.

Charles I is said to haunt the Court House, Painswick, because it was in this house that he ordered the Siege of Gloucester, and in the Court House gardens and grounds, ghostly cavaliers have been seen, flitting around, presumably getting ready for the siege.

They say there are more ghosts in Gloucestershire than you could 'shake a stick at'. I believe it!

❖

Littledean's Haunted Heritage

D own in the Forest of Dean near the river Severn, you will find yet another candidate for the title of 'Most Haunted House in England'. But the stark, forbidding mansion of Littledean can certainly also claim that according to the *Guinness Book of Records* it is probably the oldest continuously inhabited English house. It has evolved and developed over the centuries from a Saxon hall built over the ruins of a Roman temple, believed to be a shrine to Sabrina, the river goddess, and its situation where several ley lines intersect and its often violent past may have a significant influence on Littledean's history of paranormal happenings.

At the time of the Civil War in 1644, Royalist troops using the Hall as their headquarters were involved in a fierce swordfight with Parliamentarians and the Royalists who were slaughtered left bloodstains on the dining room floor, said to be impossible to remove, even after floorboards were replaced.

Until the end of the 19th century the house was owned by generations of the Pyrke family, and Littledean saw yet another tragedy when two Pyrke brothers shot each other across the dining room table with duelling pistols when they found they were both in love with the same woman. And in 1741 Charles Pyrke was murdered by his previously devoted West Indian servant, when the man's sister gave birth to a black baby, reputedly fathered by Charles. The murderer was hanged, and the spirit of a young black servant has been seen on the landing, holding a candle.

Small wonder that some of its many visitors, residents and staff feel that the house has an oppressive, even hostile atmosphere. All kinds of phenomena have been witnessed, such as swirling mist, orbs of light, also sounds such as rapping, slamming doors, screams and the clash of swords and pistol shots. The various apparitions include a monk, Royalist soldiers and a lady seen in the haunted bedroom. Smells vary from the pleasant scent of roses to the nauseating smell of decaying flesh, and some people sensitive to the atmosphere in the house have reported dizziness, nausea and palpitations, while others are aware of cold spots, and have even felt themselves pushed or punched by unseen hands.

A former employee had a frightening experience in the tea room in the 1990s when she noticed 'a sort of black mist' emerge billowing from a crack in the wall. As she watched, it formed into a dark mass which wrapped itself around her, and she felt she was physically prevented from moving. Then suddenly she felt herself given a strong push and found herself out of it.

The house is, of course, a target for paranormal researchers, some equipped with the latest high-tech spectre-detecting equipment although this is often unsuccessful in contacting the supernatural. A clergyman who visited Littledean a few years ago was so concerned about the oppressive presence he was aware of that he asked to be allowed to perform a cleansing ritual in an attempt to exorcise the malevolent influence in the house. He conducted his ritual and afterwards those present could definitely feel a lifting of the atmosphere.

Since the 1950s the house has belonged to the Macer-Wright family,

Littledean Hall – is this the most haunted house in England?

and Donald Macer-Wright, who grew up there sharing his home with its many paranormal manifestations, tried to sell it in 1991 without success. He has said that the very look and feel of Littledean creates an expectation of supernatural phenomena and it is tempting to attribute every unusual occurrence to ghosts. But he has been wakened by the sounds of clashing swords, and on another occasion when the barking of his dog aroused him, he sat up in bed and suddenly felt such a hard push in his back that he was thrown across the bed. There was no one to be seen in the room.

Littledean, in the mysterious and beautiful Forest of Dean, is a place where it is easy to conjure up images of times past. Its often violent and tragic history seems to have left psychic traces in the very air of this strange old house.

HAMPSHIRE

Down in the Forest ...

We only ever knew him as 'the captain'. His workplace had been the world's oceans. Now he enjoyed retirement in his home town of Lymington, where most evenings he could be found at the pub, sitting quietly over a pint in his favourite corner. Despite spending most of his life at sea, the captain had forgotten more about the New Forest than most people will ever know, which is why he was able to tell us about a bizarre forest mystery – the tall man who somehow managed to be in three places at once.

Our conversation in the pub one evening had drifted into speculation about events unusual, improbable or downright inexplicable. From there it was a short step to the supernatural. Someone recalled that more than half of all recorded 'ghosts' are actually apparitions of living individuals, not dead ones. Apparently, a full ten per cent of people who took part in a major survey claimed to have seen a ghost at some time in their lives. That in itself was remarkable. But most of them recognised the phantom as someone who was alive at the time, somewhere else. So is it possible, we wondered, for the image of a living person to be transmitted through space – a kind of natural television?

That was when the captain invited himself into our conversation. There was a funny business at Brook before the war that could have been just like that, he said. Then he told us as much of the tale as he could remember, after which we had to agree it was indeed a peculiar affair.

Perhaps detecting a touch of scepticism in his audience, he added, 'You don't have to accept my word for it. The newspapers wrote about it at the time.' And he was right. Several years later I came across an old article by E.A. Mitchell, a seasoned journalist who wrote a weekly column for the *Southern Daily Echo* under the pseudonym of 'Townsman'. His headline shot me back in time. 'Were These People Real?' it asked, and beneath that: 'The Tall Man of Brook ...'

The strange story reported by Mitchell was almost exactly as the captain had remembered. It happened between the wars, a period when people routinely undertook quite lengthy bicycle journeys, private motor transport being a rarity. Betty Bone, a young woman possibly in her late teens or early twenties, was staying in Breamore, a village near Fordingbridge in the New Forest. She sometimes cycled to Southampton to visit her family, a round trip of some 32 miles. Unfortunately, her journeys along the quiet forest roads had been spoiled recently by a band of gypsies who demanded money from passers-by and threatened violence when refused. Hearing about this upon her arrival in Southampton one weekend in May 1924, her father arranged for Betty to be escorted back to Breamore by her brother and his friend, Ewart Pope. They too are pictured in the newspaper and appear to have been in her age bracket.

It was a fine, clear Sunday evening when the three young people set off from Southampton on their bicycles. Twilight was still an hour or so away as they cycled past Cadnam to pick up the road that runs through the New Forest to Fordingbridge. Nowadays it's the B3078. Nothing seemed untoward until they were opposite the entrance to Brimshaw golf links, roughly a quarter of a mile beyond the Bell Inn at Brook. The road was empty; there were few motor vehicles on minor forest roads in those days. Visibility was good, even though the cyclists were coming up to an avenue of trees, so they were startled to find themselves suddenly about to overtake a man who was walking in their same direction.

Several things were unusual. In the first place, for some strange reason none of them had noticed the pedestrian until they were only about 20 yards from him. 'He just appeared,' was how they described it. Next, his height. They all agreed later that the man was exceptionally tall – at least seven feet, said one of the trio. No, he was even taller than that, thought another, so lofty it seemed he must have been on stilts. Then there was his clothing. The tall man was wearing a long coat, similar it seems to a frock coat (we are told it suggested certain pictures of the Charles Dickens character, Mr Micawber), and a tall, brimmed hat, like an antiquated top hat.

Striding purposefully in the direction of Fordingbridge, he was certainly a peculiar sight. For all that, the three young people sailed past him on their cycles without glancing back, so none of them saw his face. That might have been the end of the matter had not a curious event followed.

They had travelled roughly another quarter of a mile and were approaching the top of Telegraph Hill – when precisely the same thing happened. From nowhere, it seemed, the tall man was there again, about 20 paces ahead on a clear road and still walking steadily forwards. From his height and clothing there was no doubt that he was the identical man they had passed previously. But of course it was impossible. There was no way he could have overtaken them. They would have noticed him and anyway their speed was much greater than his.

Understandably, his sudden reappearance shook the trio, who all confessed later to having felt a sense of unease as they pedalled past at quite a pace. Again, none of them saw his face. But an even greater surprise awaited them further up the road. About a quarter of a mile beyond Telegraph Hill, which was where they had passed the man for the second time, the forest gave way to almost completely open country with very few trees bordering the road, making visibility even better than before. It was not twilight, let alone dusk. The three cyclists were approaching a crossroads where the left turn leads to Fritham and the right to Nomansland when, to their utter amazement, he suddenly appeared in front of them for a third time.

One moment they were cycling along a road that was empty as far as the eye could see, the next they were behind the same tall man as he strode in a determined manner towards some distant destination. And, as on the previous two occasions, the mystery figure appeared to be as substantial as any mortal man.

A contemporary drawing showing the Tall Man of Brook near the entrance to Bramshaw golf course

How was it possible for one person to be in three places at virtually the same time? And how could he suddenly appear in their path where previously they had seen nothing? All three later agreed that this was the moment they became thoroughly alarmed and pedalled furiously to get past the strange being in the shortest possible time.

Having delivered Betty Bone safely at Breamore, the two young men braved the return journey through the darkening forest. Although in later years they were able to laugh as they told their tale, they admitted that at the time their nerves were on edge. Even when the lamp fell from one of their bicycles they preferred to pedal on, rather than to stop and pick it up.

Who or what was the Tall Man of Brook? No one knows. There have been no further recorded sightings, but when interviewed 14 years later the three cyclists, by then married and with no cause to maintain any pretence, remained adamant that for a few minutes on a lonely forest road they had encountered something entirely baffling.

THE ISLE OF WIGHT

Lucy Lightfoot and the Crusader

This is a strange and fascinating story which leaves the reader with many questions and no answers. Its hero is Edward Estur, a knight whose family, lords of the manor at Gatcombe in the Isle of Wight, built the church of St Olave in the 13th century, as a family chapel. Over the centuries many additions and alterations have been made to the building where now Edward Estur's handsome armour-clad effigy, carved in solid oak, lies. His legs are crossed, a sign that he was a knight who fought in the Crusades, and his feet rest on a small dog.

Eighteenth century engravings show him holding a short steel dagger, known as a misericord, its hilt set with a chrysoberyl jewel encased in a lodestone mount. But today, this weapon is a wooden replica, the original said to have been damaged on the fateful morning of 13th June 1831 when certain curious events occurred.

Our heroine was born at Stoney Meadow Farm in Bowcombe, about two miles from Gatcombe, and in her early twenties Lucy Lightfoot was a beautiful, lively young girl and a keen horsewoman. She had attended St Olave's church regularly on Sundays for some years, but could often be seen there at other times as well, and it was noticed that she had apparently become obsessed with Edward Estur's effigy. She would stand totally absorbed, staring into his face, and when asked why, her answer was: 'I love to be with him and accompany him on his adventures in my thoughts and dreams.'

No doubt there were some who thought it unnatural that such a lovely young girl should waste her romantic fantasies on a centuries old monument rather than a flesh and blood admirer, and there were many whose hearts were captured by her, but to no avail.

Edward Estur lies in Gatcombe church, still clutching his dagger – now a wooden replacement added since 13th June 1831

On 13th June in 1831 Lucy arrived on horseback at the church at about 10.30 am, tethered her horse at the gate, and went into the church as she had so often done before. Shortly afterwards, at 11 am, there was a total eclipse of the sun, with darkness lasting for more than half an hour, while an extraordinarily violent storm burst upon the island causing floods and great damage, and many properties were struck by lightning. Nothing to equal the ferocity of the storm, combined with the eclipse had ever happened before on the island within living memory.

It was two or three hours later that a farmer, George Brewster, came by the church and saw Lucy's horse, frightened and distressed, still standing tethered to the gate. He went into the church expecting to find Lucy inside, but there was no sign of her, so he looked round the churchyard and made enquiries to see if she was sheltering in one of the nearby cottages.

But Lucy was nowhere to be found, and despite widespread searches and a subsequent large reward offered by her distraught parents, no clues to her disappearance ever came to light. She had vanished without trace!

But there was one curious thing noticed by the rector. The metal misericord had been torn from the hand of Edward Astur's effigy, and lay broken on the altar, the jewel set in its hilt now gone.

In more recent times the Rev James Evans, a former rector of St Olave's church, wrote the story of Lucy Lightfoot, and described how in 1865 a Methodist minister of the Scilly Isles, the Rev Samuel Trelawney, had been researching the history of the Crusades when he came across a manuscript by Phillipe de Mezieres, Chancellor to the King of Cyprus, which included a list of the names of English knights who had joined Peter I in his battle to destroy the hold of the Mamelukes on the Holy Land. Among them was the name of Edward Estur, who was said to be accompanied by a brave and beautiful young woman, by name – Lucy Lightfoot of Carisbrooke!

The story goes that the knights and Lucy travelled to Cyprus in 1365, where although she, too, had hoped to go with them to the Holy Land, she was persuaded to remain while the Crusaders went on to Alexandria, which they conquered in October. They then went on to ravage the coast of Syria where Edward was seriously wounded in the head by a Saracen, and lay dangerously ill before eventually he was brought home, both health and memory gone.

King Peter of Cyprus rewarded the Crusaders who had come to his aid with the Order of the Sword, a silver bejewelled dagger, the same no doubt as the one in the hand of Edward Estur's effigy. We are not told how long Edward survived but the Saracen's sword had caused serious damage and shortened his life, and he died at home in Gatcombe.

But what of Lucy after Edward departed on his fateful journey? It is said that she waited three years for her lover to return, then believing him to be dead, she ultimately left Cyprus for Corsica where she married a fisherman, Lionallo Marnellino. She lived a long, hardworking life, helping her husband with his fishing, and growing citrus fruit and grapes, and leaving a large family of children and grandchildren when she finally died at a considerable age.

So what really happened during that terrific storm on the morning of 13th June 1831 when the 19th century Lucy Lightfoot paid one of her frequent visits to the tomb of Edward Estur? Is it conceivable that in some kind of time warp two lovers were reunited over the centuries?

As the Rev James Evans wrote in his booklet, 13th June 1831 was no ordinary day. There was a unique combination of a tropical storm and a total eclipse, and he also points out the significance of the crystal in the dagger. When crystals disintegrate under pressure, he says, tremendous forces are released which could, perhaps, distort time itself. There are many instances where people have found themselves suddenly switched to another earlier time, before just as suddenly returning to the present.

Did something like that happen to Lucy Lightfoot, except that in her case, she did not return? As the Rev James Evans so charmingly puts it: 'Thus Lucy Lightfoot just stepped lightly into the past and stayed as she always longed with her loved one.'

HEREFORDSHIRE

The Haunted River Wye

T he Wye has its own ghost stories, often uneasily recalled at night by superstitious boatmen. One concerns Goodrich Castle, a few miles from Ross-on-Wye, which was besieged by Cromwell's men under Colonel John Birch in 1646 during the Civil War.

The Colonel's niece, Alice Birch, had taken refuge in the castle with her Royalist lover, Charles Clifford, and the two of them tried to make their escape on horseback, but the Wye was in spate at the time, and both were drowned. This tragedy took place on or around 14th June, and people have reported sightings of the lovers' ghosts at this time plunging into the river on their white stallion.

The stretch of the Wye which runs through Hampton Bishop, south of Hereford, has an alarming manifestation known locally as the Spectre's Voyage. This is the ghost of a woman in a small boat which, regardless of the state of the current or the wind, travels at speed to the river bank near Hampton Bishop. Once there she disembarks, crying and lamenting loudly, then back in her boat she sets off in the direction of Hereford, but suddenly disappears before she reaches the city.

The reason why local boatmen try to avoid travelling on the river at around 8 pm at night is that anyone unlucky enough to see the Spectre's Voyage is said to be destined to die soon afterwards.

Tradition has it that the ghost is Isobel Chandos, daughter of the Governor of Hereford Castle in the reign of Edward II. Her lover was hanged for treachery to the King, and Isobel, demented by grief, drowned in the Wye.

The Exorcism of Black Vaughan

Hergest Court was for centuries the traditional manor of the Vaughan family, and home of Hereford's most famous ghost, Black Vaughan. This was Thomas Vaughan, who was taken prisoner and beheaded after the Battle of Banbury in 1469. It is said that when his head fell, it was immediately seized by his faithful black bloodhound who made off with it.

Black Vaughan proved to be a restless ghost, often frightening farmers' wives on their way to market, and eventually an exorcism ceremony with the requisite twelve clergymen was arranged. Their intention was to imprison Black Vaughan's spirit in a silver snuff box, and they began their rite, each holding a lighted candle. The ghost promptly extinguished eleven of the candles, but the priest bearing the twelfth, undaunted, continued to read the exorcism. Eventually Vaughan's spirit was imprisoned and committed to Hergest Pool for a thousand years, but the exorcism does not seem to have been entirely effective as his head has been seen hovering above the moat, and both he and his dog are said to haunt the road to Kington church where Vaughan's body lies in the Vaughan chapel. The dog is also said to haunt the house and surroundings where its appearance foretells a family death.

Something Strange at the Cathedral

It's not often that a ghost makes such a well authenticated appearance, but some years ago the apparition of a White Monk chose the Three Choirs Festival to make his appearance in Hereford Cathedral, to the amazement of the many visitors.

He appeared at midnight in the north-east corner of the Cathedral, near the Lady Chapel, and it is thought he may be the ghost of a monk killed in the cathedral in 1055 by a Welshman, but history does not reveal any details of this event.

Hereford also has a 17th century haunted house with a very persistent ghost. The house was towed 100 yards down the High Street to a new position in 1966 during development in the area, but, undeterred, its former owner continued to haunt. He was an apothecary who had accidentally poisoned his apprentice and had committed suicide in remorse.

HERTFORDSHIRE

St Albans' Haunted Abbey

I t was a crisp, cold Christmas Eve as a 16 year old youth made his way up the hill towards the great Norman Abbey, standing serene in the moonlight, dominating the city of St Albans as it had for hundreds of years.

On this special night of the year people should have been flocking there for the Christmas Midnight Mass as the bells pealed out the age-old summons to celebrate the birth of Christ. But the Abbey was dark and silent, the twelve huge bells removed from the belfry, for it was 1944, England was at war, and the young man who let himself in through a side door was there as one of a team of fire-watchers. It was their job to spend the night in the Abbey in case of fire bombs, and to make a regular check of the whole building and the fire-fighting equipment. Nights like this, with what people called a 'bomber's moon', required extra vigilance.

There was no sound but his own echoing footsteps on the stone-flagged floor as Basil Saville made his way through the vast dark shadowy building to the vestry. He walked confidently for, as he had been a chorister, the Abbey was a familiar place to him, but when he discovered that no other fire-watcher had arrived, he had to admit that the thought of guarding this historic edifice on his own was a daunting prospect.

But it had to be done, so when no one else came, he set off on the regular tour of the building. It was cold and frosty outside, but the Abbey seemed even colder, with that deep penetrating chill of old churches, and the moonlight filtering faintly through the windows made the shadows even deeper.

Basil felt uneasy, something wasn't quite as it should be, and he tried to shrug off a growing feeling that although his regulation hooded torch revealed nothing untoward, he was not alone in that ancient holy place.

He followed his usual route through the Abbey, checking the water containers, stirrup pumps and hoses as he went, until he reached the Saint's Chapel where the Shrine of Saint Alban stands, and an early 15th century watching chamber from which monks used to keep a vigilant eye on pilgrims visiting the martyr's shrine.

The feeling that he, too, was being watched was very strong now, and as Basil shone his torch high up into the watching chamber he felt the hairs on the back of his neck rise as he thought he could glimpse two hooded figures. He called out, then climbed the rickety old staircase up to the loft, but his torch revealed no intruders and he knew no one could have passed him. His heart beat faster as he noticed two monks' habits lying there on the floor, but Basil tried to reassure himself that they must have been used for some theatrical production, although he could not recall anything of the kind.

He was relieved to reach the blacked out Lady Chapel where at last it was possible to switch on some light, and he sat for a while trying to collect his thoughts, conscious of the lonely emptiness around him, then continued his patrol.

On his way to the twisting staircase which led to the roof he almost fell against one of the Abbey's great bells which had been stored on the ground floor for the duration of the war. But as he climbed into the upper regions above the nave he all but lost his balance as suddenly a bell began to toll in the belfry. How could this be happening? Hadn't he nearby tripped over one of the bells down below? And yet the steady tolling went on, so summoning his courage he opened the belfry door as the sound died away and found, as he knew he would, that there were no bells hanging there.

The tolling had stopped and, confused and at a loss to understand his extraordinary experiences, Basil climbed out onto the roof of the tower, standing there in the moonlight, grateful for the cold fresh air on his face.

But the events of that strange Christmas night were not yet over. As he

St Albans Abbey, the home of glorious music – ghostly and corporeal

started back down the stairs, the organ began to play and looking towards the organ loft he saw a candle flickering by the console but could not see the organist. Instinctively he called out the fire-watcher's familiar warning – 'Put that light out' – and moved to get a better view.

There was no one seated at the organ and yet, from his vantage point above, Basil could see the pages of a book of music turning, and the organ keys being depressed by unseen fingers. Then suddenly from the direction of the high altar came a glorious burst of singing.

Hardly knowing what he was doing, Basil hurried down the stairs and through the Abbey towards the choir stalls. The music had stopped now, but as he looked towards the high altar he saw a magnificent sight. A procession of monks with their abbot, all holding candles, were leaving the high altar and passing through the screen doors into the Saint's Chapel. The doors closed behind them, and Basil followed to the chapel, only to find it empty and in darkness. He ran back and climbed up to the organ loft and, in the light of his torch, found a spent candle and a book of music. Here at least was some tangible evidence that he had not imagined the whole extraordinary experience.

The book was quite large, with plain black covers and yellowing manuscript pages. Opening it he read the title, *Albanus Mass* by Robert Fayrfax.

Back in the vestry, he was relieved to find his fellow fire-watcher had arrived. The other man had apparently heard and seen nothing, and together they went round the Abbey again, as Basil told his companion about the strange events he had witnessed. But when they reached the organ loft the used candle he had seen was no longer there, and the two monks' habits had disappeared from the floor of the watching loft.

Had it all been a dream? But after all these years the powerful impression of that wartime Christmas Eve remains with him.

'I was stunned by it - overwhelmed,' he recently told me. 'I'm not psychic or anything like that,' he added, 'and I've never seen anything like it either before or since. People may not believe me, but I know it happened.'

He wrote down his experience soon afterwards, while it was all fresh in his mind, but thinking people would not believe him, he kept it locked away in his memory and told no one. Then in 1982 he saw that the *Evening Post-Echo* were asking their readers for Christmas stories, so he sent them what he had written all those years ago, and they published it.

But although Basil Saville's experience may have been unique, this was not the first time that the apparently empty Abbey has echoed to the night music of an unseen choir.

W.B. Gerish, a local historian, who wrote about Hertfordshire ghost stories in the early part of the last century, recalled a phantom organist who was sometimes heard playing 'heavenly music' on the Abbey organ in the middle of the night. And over the years there have been reports of sightings of Benedictine monks in and around the Abbey, figures which appear quite real only to disappear disconcertingly through walls or closed doors.

For hundreds of years the Abbey was a great Benedictine ecclesiastical establishment and seat of learning. Is it surprising that shadows of the past should linger for those able to see them or that in some strange time-warp the monks of long ago still sing the mass Robert Fayrfax wrote especially for their Abbey?

Fayrfax was organist and director of the Abbey choir at the beginning of the 16th century, and he became a great man in the musical world of his day. *The Oxford Companion to Music* refers to him as the 'prime musician of the nation', and after he became Master of the King's Musick one of the highlights of his life must surely have been when he accompanied Henry VIII to France to the Field of the Cloth of Gold, where he led the royal singers.

Fayrfax died in October 1521, and about a year before the 400th anniversary of his death, a copy of his *Albanus Mass* in the old medieval notation was discovered. It was hundreds of years since it had been performed but the fortunate coincidence inspired the Abbey organist, Willie Luttmann, to transcribe it and on 30th October 1921 it was performed at a commemorative concert at the Abbey.

The morning after the concert Mr Frank Drakard of Harpenden had some business with Canon Glossop, who lived in Romeland House, close by the Abbey, and some years ago he told me of their conversation.

'Did you enjoy the Fayrfax music last night, Canon?' 'Yes,' replied the Canon, 'but you know, Drakard, I had heard it before.'

Surprised, Mr Drakard asked, 'Do you mean when they were practising?'

'No,' said the Canon, 'I have heard it in the middle of the night on more than one occasion. The first time was when I was returning home very late, and I got one of my daughters up also and we went out of doors and listened to it. When I heard it in the Abbey last night, I recognised it. I also know there was no human choir in the Abbey at the times we heard it in the night.'

'Knowing Canon Glossop as I did for a most level-headed and matter-of-fact man,' added Mr Drakard, 'I absolutely believed him.'

Dr Elsie Toms, St Albans historian, was told by Canon Glossop's daughter that one night she got out of bed to fetch a drink for a young relative who was staying with them. She heard the sound of men's voices singing in the street outside, but when she looked out of the window there was nothing to see.

She told her father, who was working late in his study, and when they both went outside the unseen procession of singers appeared to pass by and continue towards the Abbey, only a stone's throw away. The Abbey gate was locked so they could not follow, but the sound went on as if the singers had entered the Abbey by the main entrance.

From time to time other people have heard music as they passed the Abbey late at night. One local resident told me that when she was a young girl in 1938 she and a friend passed by the Abbey in the late evening, and hearing 'really wonderful' music they peeped inside. But when they found the building dark and empty, they were afraid and hurried off home as fast as possible!

But as ghost stories go, the heavenly choir of St Albans Abbey is charming rather than alarming. Long may they sing.

A King's Mistress Still Lingers ...

T here was something oddly disturbing about the tall young man who had appeared so suddenly by the coach house. Perhaps it was his clothes, although the frilly white shirt and dark knee breeches would not have been out of place on a pop singer. There were large shiny buckles on his shoes, and his long fair hair was tied back in a pony tail.

He looked intently at the startled girl, the hint of a smile on his handsome, rather serious young face. But as she looked back at him, feeling uneasy without quite knowing why, she realised that he was beginning to look more and more like a faded photograph. He was disappearing in front of her eyes.

Maria Goldsmith was the girl, and we met in the Tudor cottage where she lived with her husband Robin in the grounds of Salisbury Hall, one of the most haunted houses in the country. The stormy wind outside made the old rafters creak like a ship at sea, but inside it was warm and comfortable with its white walls, oak beams and the soft hiss of a log fire.

Although Maria had lived in the village close by the Hall, she had never heard the ghost stories connected with it, so her meeting with the young Cavalier had the double impact of terror and surprise.

'It was in the summer,' she told me, 'at about half past ten at night. It was still quite light. I remember Robin and I were at the moat, and like a couple of children we started playing hide and seek round the coach house when suddenly I noticed this chap.

'He was very old-fashioned in the way he was dressed, which made me look again. Then as I looked, he seemed to get hazy, and I realised what it must be. I'm afraid I screamed in terror. Robin came rushing down the stairs of the coach house, but he didn't see anything.'

For many years there have been stories about the ghost of a Cavalier being seen in the Hall. Apparently he was carrying secret despatches at the time of the Civil War when he encountered a party of Roundheads, and took refuge in the Hall, with his enemies close behind him. He reached the upper floors, looking desperately for a hiding place but realised too late that there was no escape, and rather than be taken, he killed himself. Some say his ghost has been seen with a sword sticking through him, others that he shot himself.

Robin Goldsmith told me that the passage where the ghost walks used to run right through the house into the Tudor wing, now demolished. Many people, including Robin's mother, had heard footsteps at night passing along the passage when no one else was there.

Lady Gresley, wife of Sir Nigel Gresley, designer of the record-breaking Pacific steam locomotives, lived at the Hall in the Thirties and had the terrifying experience of actually seeing the Cavalier's ghost enter her bedroom one night. She was so frightened that she never slept in that room again. Was this the young Cavalier that Maria encountered? It seems likely that this may have been a different manifestation.

At the time of Maria's ghostly visitation Robin's family lived in Salisbury Hall itself, a lovely mellow old house near London Colney, with a long history and many memorable owners over the centuries. A narrow lane turning off from the B556 road between London and St Albans leads to an ancient medieval bridge, fording the moat which surrounds this peaceful oasis, set in rolling farmland with a distant view of St Albans Abbey.

When the Goldsmith family made Salisbury Hall their home it was almost derelict and overgrown with brambles, and it was a labour of love to restore and furnish it. They found that gardening was something of an archaeological treasure hunt as relics of earlier times came to light, and a growing collection of old coins, buckles, spurs, broken remnants of swords and ancient tiles told their own story of a past which seems very close there.

The Domesday Book records a Saxon manor on the site, and at the time of the Wars of the Roses, the great Warwick the Kingmaker, resplendent in his Lancastrian armour, rode out in 1471 from the manor, then simply called Salisbury's, to defeat and death in the Battle of Barnet. Later, Henry VIII's treasurer built himself a fine mansion there, of which little remains.

But perhaps Salisbury Hall's most interesting memories belong to the time when it was the setting for one of the most romantic liaisons of history. The Hall was bought secretly on behalf of Charles II the year his love affair with Nell Gwynn began, and extensive improvements and alterations were soon under way to turn the house into a royal hideaway, far from the intrigues and prying eyes of the Court, where the Merry Monarch could snatch a little summer love with his beloved Nell.

The flint and brick building beside the moat has always been known as Nell Gwynn's cottage, and when Robin and Maria got married they decided to make their home there.

It is believed that Nell Gwynn's first son was born at Salisbury Hall, and was looked after by nurses in the cottage. Maria and I opened the little diamond paned window in the cottage bedroom and looked down to the moat below.

'This is where Nell Gwynn is supposed to have held her baby out of the window and threatened to throw him into the moat if Charles didn't give him a title,' said Maria. 'Charles, perhaps inspired by the sight of St Albans Abbey across the fields, said "Pray spare the Duke of St Albans".'

Nell Gwynn is Salisbury Hall's most famous ghost, and there have been sightings of King Charles's pretty mistress in one of the bedrooms and in the panelled Crown Chamber downstairs.

Winston Churchill's beautiful mother Jenny once lived at Salisbury Hall with her second husband, George Cornwallis-West. In those days, the cream of Edwardian society danced in the ballroom, now vanished, and the singer Dame Nellie Melba, the great actress Eleanora Duse, and Edward VII were also among the visitors. In fact, Winston found his lively mother's social whirl too much at times, and would escape to his tree house in a tall lime at the back of the house where he could retreat to read and write his speeches in peace.

George Cornwallis-West once saw an unknown young woman standing at the foot of the stairs. She looked at him intently, then turned and went through the door into a passage, and puzzled, he followed, but she had disappeared. Although sceptical about ghosts until then, he realised that this was no ordinary visitor. In fact, her resemblance to a maid at his mother's home made him feel afraid that something might have happened to the girl.

However, enquiries reassured him. Everything was fine, in fact the maid was just on the point of getting married! It was sometime later, when looking at a picture of Nell Gwynn, that he noticed the striking resemblance between Nell and his mother's maid, and realised who the mysterious lady must have been.

I asked Robin Goldsmith if he had had any supernatural experiences at Salisbury Hall. He laughed, and said, 'I slept in the little room over the porch for seven years, and I didn't see or hear a thing.'

This room had an eerie reputation for many years. 'I used to stay in the house sometimes when Robin and I were engaged,' remarked Maria, 'and one night I slept in the room over the porch as there was no other room available.

'I had a terrible feeling when I first went in. I hadn't heard anything about the room being haunted, I just felt I wanted to get away, and went to bed feeling quite miserable. There was a clock in there that chimed every hour, so Robin stopped it in case it woke me up.

'Well, I did wake up! It was about 2 am and the first thing I noticed was that the clock was ticking away merrily again. Then the bed began to rock quite violently back and forth for about three minutes.

'You can imagine', she continued with a reminiscent shudder, 'how I huddled under the bedclothes, absolutely paralysed with fear. I thought I must be dreaming. I got up next morning at about six. I couldn't wait to get out of there, but I didn't say a word to anybody. I thought they'd think I was mad.

'But in the end I told Robin's mother what had happened, and she showed me a book which says that about the time of the First World War, a governess slept there, and that "something terrifying" came out of the wall in the night, and approached her bed. Apparently she was too scared to sleep in the house again.'

When I had visited Salisbury Hall previously, I thought that one part of the garden had a particularly serene and happy atmosphere. I mentioned this to Maria. 'Yes,' she said, 'that is where they hear the laughter.'

Apparently at times people have heard the echoes of a lovely rich laugh floating across the garden. Is it Nell Gwynn? Somehow the past seems very close at Salisbury Hall, and I feel sure Nell was happy here once long ago ... and perhaps she still comes back sometimes.

Note: Unfortunately Salisbury Hall is no longer open to the public as it is now occupied as business premises. Access is still available to the Mosquito Aircraft Museum in the grounds. The Hall was a secret aircraft design centre in the Second World War where the first Mosquito was designed and built in 1940.

KENT

The Bromley Poltergeist

O ne of the most sensational of all poltergeist cases, significant for its
curious location, its duration and its violence, occurred in Bromley.
It is further remarkable in that the three men who were subjected to such
a prolonged and alarming series of attacks decided to keep an account of
events and these, along with the records made during investigations
carried out by members of the Society for Psychical Research, make for
fascinating reading. The disturbances occurred over an unusually
prolonged two-year period on the Grove Park allotments, mainly in the
two sheds of the Kentish Garden Guild which was run by three men. This
was no mammoth business enterprise. The two adjoining sheds with their
corrugated iron roofs and their barbed wire fences were perhaps typical
of what one might expect of such a small enterprise set on waste ground
among housing estates.

Alfred Taylor, a 78 year old pensioner keeping himself active, used to
order whatever was necessary each Thursday and on Sunday morning he
and his two colleagues, Tony Elms and Clifford Jewiss, sold the various
items to other allotment holders. It was on one of those Sunday mornings,
26th April 1973, that the first curious incident occurred. This was a day on
which Taylor felt that Elms was upset about something. It is worth
bearing that in mind. But there was never anything to tie the 50 year old
Elms (or, indeed, either of the others) into the disturbances, nothing to
suggest that his mental or psychic state gave some kind of impetus to the
succession of incredible happenings at Grove Park.

What happened was out of the blue. The men were in the trading shed
when some powder suddenly hit the ceiling. They all looked at it. Kids up
to some mischief? Some sort of prank? That was certainly Clifford Jewiss's
first thought. Then a small pewter jug on a cupboard shelf suddenly shot

across the floor. Even then no one quite took in what was happening. You can buy all sorts of tricks in joke shops. But after Jewiss picked up the jug and put it in a box with a lid they had cause to think again, for the jug was on the floor once more. And the lid of the box was still in place. Matter cannot pass through matter, anybody knows that. But the jug ...?

Over the following weeks there was a succession of inexplicable happenings. Out of the bin of Growmore fertiliser came fountains of pellets, hitting the ceiling, sometimes showering onto customers. On one occasion a 7lb weight sailed off the scales and round Alf Taylor's head. Sometimes all manner of items left their places one after another, though no one ever saw them take off. But they watched them, in Taylor's words, 'going round the hut like skittles.' None of the men could understand what was really happening. They tried sometimes to persuade themselves that they were victims of some kind of elaborate hoax but they could not really be convinced of this for the whole exhibition – that is quite a good description of what they were observing so regularly – was too complex to be the result of human agency. Objects were acting as though they had a life of their own.

And this was so damaging to business. It was proving to be extremely costly. Bottles were unscrewed and their contents were poured out on the floor of the shed. The taps of tubs of liquid Maxicrop were turned on. More than 1 cwt of Growmore pellets was lost from the storage bins and remarkably it seemed as if human hands had scooped them out for on the surface of the remaining pellets in one of the tubs there were the impressions of fingers. But no one could easily get at the bins without being seen. How could these be human hands?

It was the general nuisance, the spiteful nature of some of the tricks, that upset the men. Money was taken from one of their cars and later coins fell from the ceiling. Other coins fastened inside plastic bags fell out of their own accord. When Tony Elms was about to drink coffee out of a mug the contents escaped and were replaced with fertiliser.

Elms was a frequent target. He was to say later: 'It frightened me. I've seen a half-ton bag of fertiliser move. The whole building would shake sometimes. Money would fly about and I've seen 7lb bags of fertiliser move from the shelf and hit customers.' There was an occasion when the men had to abandon business before 1 pm, the usual closing time, because the objects were moving as fast as they were replaced.

One of the customers, pensioner George Bentley, recalled: 'One time some money disappeared and the next thing I knew a 10p coin fell into a cup of tea I was drinking. Another time I went into the shed to buy a 7lb bag of Growmore. I asked for it and I saw it lift off the shelf, float across and burst open on the counter. There were some right queer goings on and a lot of us saw them.'

The success of the business was undoubtedly imperilled by the manic activities of the poltergeist. Something had to be done. It was Elms who asked for help from an unspecified group of either churchmen or white magicians. Following their advice he carried out a DIY exorcism alone in the darkness of one of the sheds. Outside, the others could hear bangings so loud that they feared that the walls would collapse. Nine times the heavy iron door swung open as if subjected to massive blows. At the end Tony Elms came out, his head cut and his hand heavily bruised.

But the exorcism – did it work? When the men went back on the Saturday evening to prepare for the next day's sales, the interior of the shed looked 'as if it had been hit by a bomb'. The goods were all thrown off the shelves and circled them in constant motion. All over the walls, on all of the surfaces in the sheds, on chairs, benches, tubs and bins, the sign of the cross was scratched, painted, shaped in drawing pins and drawn. Two large planks (5ft 6in) which had been used to barricade the sheds vanished completely one day. The next day when Taylor and Elms arrived at the allotments, there were the missing planks arranged in the shape of a cross. It seemed a conscious mockery of Tony Elms and his attempt to exorcise the sprit that so plagued him and his colleagues.

Alf Taylor was attacked away from the premises and in the presence of witnesses in his own home. On another occasion he claimed that he was pushed in Bromley Council Offices. So it did seem that whatever it was that made life such a misery was not solely active in one place.

In September 1973 Alf Taylor rang the Society for Psychical Research, asking for help. Manfred Cassirer, Chairman of the Physical Phenomena Committee, and his wife and fellow researcher, Pauline Runnells, met Taylor in his house at Downham and agreed to visit the site. What they saw convinced them that the men were not making up a story. And why should they? The wretched affair was costing them money.

The researchers paid two visits, one in October 1973 and a second in June 1974. The reason for the interval was the reluctance on the part of the three men to delve further into the mysteries. But on their two visits Manfred Cassirer and Pauline Runnells saw the whole remarkable display of tricks and more. They saw security bolts disappear from a window to be rediscovered inside a car outside. In front of them Tony Elms had a saw rammed down his back and his shirt ripped. As they stood inside the building, it was shaken by what seemed to be a series of angry blows.

The number 1659 – a date? a code? – appeared on a wooden panel, the consequence of automatic writing. It looked to be written in blood though had it been analysed perhaps it would have proved to be Maxicrop. And there was more writing and further scrawls – a large question mark; assorted letters of the alphabet; the name of one of Taylor's friends.

On the second visit there were two particularly notable features. There were the usual instances of teleportation. Nothing was safe. A watering can took off; a bottle of ant killer had to be replaced three times on a shelf; wooden planks fell down; a bottle appeared to be suspended in mid-air; and on a shelf what at first sight appeared to be the impression of a child's hand changed imperceptibly into a face yet – and this is the eerie part – the actual movements of the change could not be seen. At first it was a hand, then a face. Then from the counter a rectangular brass object stamped MN dropped onto the floor. But what was it? Where had it come from? None of the men claimed to have seen it before; none of them could interpret MN. It was as though it had come from another world.

Then there was another weird manifestation. Before the two researchers arrived a face, of human proportions, took shape on the counter. Made from two chemicals in the shed, its features, outlined in white sulphite, were like a skull. The eyes, nose and mouth were represented by brown Maxicrop. It could not have been made by any of the men. It required skill as well as speed. None of them had either the ability or the time to fashion so curious a piece of artwork. Then before the eyes of all five, allotment holders and observers, the face gradually changed, wore away, wasted, and again no actual movement was seen though all watched its deterioration.

What else? Oh, disappearing car keys; Taylor's missing thermos flask which was found in a carrier bag on Jewiss's motor cycle; £4 of the day's takings lost; a gardening fork returned to the shed after disappearing; fertiliser instead of coffee appearing in a thermos flask; money found inside plastic bags; Elms pushed violently into Cassirer and later almost choked on a flower bulb sticking out of his mouth. What a memorable couple of visits for Cassirer and Runnells.

The visits of the researchers did not call a halt to the activities of the Bromley poltergeist. But stop they did some months later, just as suddenly as they began. The whole wicked, insanely childish behaviour came to an end. 'It all stopped after work on a new block of garages was finished', according to George Bentley.

Where did it come from, this vandal, this malicious entity? According to one school of thought, poltergeists have their source in the living, in the very personalities who are under siege, and do not spring from the dead. There is the sense of something hidden in a living personality, something waiting to be triggered. But why did it select Tony Elms more frequently than his two colleagues? Was there something in his subconscious self, in his personality? Was there some hidden story, some concealed anger somewhere, some burning resentment? Was he the source or was he simply the target? Did this activity emerge from a deep hidden level? Was it some unsuspected turmoil, some unknown disturbance in either of the other men? Certainly, the affair distressed and mystified all of them. Each of them would have been horrified to think himself the source of this frightening and inexplicable activity.

But what a mystery it is. What an unnerving mystery.

Time-Slips

I magine ... you pass an acquaintance in the street and give a wave. Your acquaintance acknowledges you. He is going in the opposite direction. You immediately turn the corner and here is your acquaintance coming towards you once more. But this is impossible, for you saw him further back and going in the opposite direction only seconds earlier. He could not have arrived where he now is. To do that he would have had to turn back, run past you without your seeing him and then turn round and appear once more walking towards you. Or like some superhuman athlete he has raced round several streets to come face to face with you again. Or he has a double perhaps ... well, that is possible. He had a double though you never knew that. And remarkably, the double is only yards ahead of your acquaintance. Unless of course it is the double you are now seeing ... and isn't it strange that they are wearing identical clothes. And the second figure, now that he is up to you, also acknowledges your wave. No, this is without any doubt your friend.

There are several cases of this kind on record and it is reckoned that some kind of slippage in time has taken place. Imagine time to be something like a piece of string held out taut and we move along it at the same pace. But, say this straight length of string somehow loses its tautness, that it gets a loop in it. What if time sometimes does this? It may be a highly unscientific way of describing time but perhaps it helps us to understand what might have happened when you twice met your friend in the street. Either he or you somehow walked round the loop.

Enough of trying to describe time-slips. Here is a fascinating illustration from Tunbridge Wells. On the morning of 18th June 1968, an elderly lady, Mrs Charlotte Warburton, went shopping with her husband in the town. They decided to go their separate ways for a while and to meet up later. Unable to find a particular brand of coffee from her usual grocer she went into a supermarket in Calverley Road. As she entered the shop she saw a small café through an entrance in the left-hand wall. She had never before realised that there was a café there. It was rather old-fashioned with wood panelled walls. There were no windows and the room was lit by a number of electric bulbs with frosted shades. There was at the time, she thought, nothing especially odd about the scene. 'Two women in rather long dresses were sitting at one table and about half a dozen men, all in dark lounge suits, were sitting at other tables further back in the room,' she said. 'All the people seemed to be drinking coffee and chatting ... a normal sight for a country town at 11 o'clock in the morning.

Mrs Warburton did not stay but she certainly did not recognise anything amiss either then or indeed for several days. Even the rather formal and slightly off-key clothing made no immediate impression on her. Nor did the fact that although the customers were talking there was no noise from them that caused her to question her senses. Nor did she notice that there was no smell of coffee.

There is clearly something strange here. Yet without questioning the circumstances in which she found herself, Mrs Warburton blithely left the café and went to meet her husband. And she did not suggest to him that the scene in the café seemed in any way odd.

When they came to Tunbridge Wells on their next shopping expedition Mrs Warburton decided to take her husband to the café. Or rather she hoped to take him there. But of course they never did find the place though they searched the street up and down. No, they were told in the supermarket, there was no café there. She must be in the wrong building. It was then that they learned about the Kosmos Kinema which had stood on the site of the supermarket. It had had a small café. They were directed to the Tunbridge Wells Constitutional Club where the steward told them that at one time the Constitutional Club had owned the premises adjoining the Kosmos which was now incorporated into the supermarket. The club had had an assembly room in those days and to the rear a small bar with tables for refreshments. Mrs Warburton's description tallied exactly with the club's old refreshment room.

The bar, the cinema and the assembly room had all vanished years ago, Mrs Warburton was told. Yet, on 18th June 1968, she had stepped into the past and like others involved in time-slips had accepted without question the place in which she found herself. Retrospective clairvoyance, it is called. Whatever it is, it is mighty odd to contemplate.

Another time-slip incident took place in Kent some years earlier. In 1935 Dr E.G. Moon, a very down-to-earth Scots physician with a practice in Broadstairs, was at Minster in Thanet visiting his patient, Lord Carson, who lived at Cleve Court. After talking to Carson, the doctor left his patient and made his way downstairs into the hallway. His mind was clearly very occupied at the time with the instructions he had given the nurse about the prescription he had left for Carson. At the front door Dr Moon hesitated, wondering whether to go back upstairs to have another word with the nurse.

It was at this point that the doctor noted that his car was no longer where he had left it in the driveway. In fact, it had been parked alongside a thick yew hedge and that too was missing. Even the drive down which he had driven from the main road was now nothing but a muddy track, and a man was coming towards him.

The newcomer on the scene, only 30 yards from Dr Moon, was rather oddly dressed, wearing an old-fashioned coat with several capes around the shoulders. And he wore a top hat of the kind seen in the previous century. As he walked he smacked a switch against his riding boots. Over his shoulder he carried a long-barrelled gun. He stared hard at Moon. And the doctor registered the fact that the man coming towards him might have looked more at home in the 19th century.

Remarkably, Dr Moon seems not at the time to have been either alarmed or even mildly surprised by the changed scenery, by the quite oddly dressed man approaching him or the fact that his car was missing. What preoccupied him was the thought of Lord Carson's prescription. He simply turned away, without any concern, to go back into the house. But he did quite casually take one more look at the scene he was leaving. And now, as if by magic, the car was back where it had been and the yew hedge too. The drive was no longer a muddy track. And the man had also disappeared, back one assumes to the previous century. And it was only now that Dr Moon realised that something odd, something decidedly odd, had occurred.

All of this took seconds and so there is every reason to understand why Dr Moon did not immediately go out into the driveway to see where his missing car was. For the same reason it is understandable why he did not speak to the man dressed like a farm bailiff of the past. Dr Moon was drawn into some kind of accepting, hallucinatory state. When he came to – for that seems to be the best way of describing his return to his own time – he described to Lady Carson what he thought had occurred. He was anxious, however, that no word of it should come out in his lifetime for fear that his patients would begin to question his judgement. It was only after his death that the story was revealed.

It is difficult to grapple with the notion of time-slips. It may be that all past events are impressed into the fabric of buildings and that in some way and on some occasions they are released. In other words, what Mrs Warburton and Dr Moon saw were ghosts but not solely of people but of all of their surroundings.

Or did Mrs Warburton and Dr Moon actually return to a real, physical past? Did they turn up as strangers, were they really the interlopers, at somebody else's present? And if so – and this is an intriguing yet unanswerable question – did some people drinking coffee one Saturday morning in a Tunbridge Wells café look up and see Mrs Warburton? Did a man dressed like a farm bailiff, walking towards Cleve Court one day well over a hundred years earlier, see a strangely dressed doctor at the front door of the house? Did the coffee drinkers ever wonder where the elderly lady had so suddenly gone? And did the farm bailiff ask himself how the oddly dressed figure in the doorway had so suddenly disappeared?

Strangely, Tunbridge Wells has thrown up another odd story that may or not have been a time-slip. This tale goes back to some time in the mid 19th century and it took place in the Swan Hotel in The Pantiles. Mrs Nancy Fuller and her young daughter, Naomi, on a first visit to the town, took a room at the top of the hotel, the room now Number 16. As they climbed the stairs to their room the girl's behaviour began to change. She appeared more and more agitated, closing her eyes and whispering to herself. When her mother asked her what was wrong Naomi replied that she recognised the stairway, that she had been there before. Then she came out with the astounding remark that her lover was waiting for her in the room as he had said he always would. When they entered the room the young girl went at once to the corner, calling out 'John' as though to someone standing there waiting. For a few seconds in her mother's eyes she seemed to change, to grow older, and even her clothing was that of an earlier time.

The story that Naomi later told her mother was that she had previously lived in this building when it was a privately owned house. This was certainly before 1835 when it became The Swan. In the days when Naomi had lived there it had been known as High House. The young girl went on to explain that she had had a love affair with a man called John but her father had disapproved, had the young man taken away and had locked her in the room. Alone in the room, aware that she would never again see him, she had conjured up the image of John and holding the hand of her imagined lover, she had jumped to her death from the window.

Room 16 is haunted. There are still tales of disarranged bed covers and of chairs being moved, and tapping at the window. Some have claimed to hear the cry 'John' carried on the wind.

But is this an early example of a time-slip? It differs from the other accounts in that Naomi was aware of a past life and her part in it. Some have regarded this story as an instance of reincarnation. Others have seen it as déja vu. But if reincarnation is the answer, what is it that triggers such an awareness of it? And if déja vu, how can that come about? It is all so complex. Perhaps it is simply a haunting resulting from a young girl's suicide. But the story is so curious that the idea of a time-slip is tempting.

LANCASHIRE

The Ghost of Birchen Bower

Hannah Beswick was a rich woman with land and a house, Birchen Bower at Hollinwood, on the outskirts of Manchester, but she was not a happy woman. Hannah was terrified of being buried alive, and this stemmed from an alarming event in her own family.

One of her brothers became ill and remained so deeply unconscious that the doctor had pronounced him dead. He was in his coffin surrounded by mourners and the funeral about to take place when he began to show signs of life, and he eventually recovered and lived for many years afterwards.

As can be imagined this made a powerful impression on Hannah and she was terrified in case something of the kind could happen to her, and she might not be rescued in time!

Her remedy was to make a will leaving all her considerable property to her doctor, Charles White, on condition that after her death her body must not be buried, but kept safely above ground, and she also specified that it should be brought back to Birchen Bower every twenty-one years, and kept there for a week.

Hannah died in 1768, and Dr White faithfully had her embalmed, coated with tar and bandaged like a mummy, with her face left uncovered as she had specified. He kept the body at his home, Sale Priory, and after his own death it was moved to Manchester's Natural History Society's Museum where it was said to be a major attraction! But in 1868, according to the *Manchester Guardian*, 'the Commissioners who are charged with the rearrangement of the Society's collection have deemed this specimen undesirable and have at last buried it.'

In the 19th century part of Birchen Bower was pulled down, and a developer converted the remaining wing into smaller dwellings which were rented out mainly to handloom weavers. Hannah's ghost had already been seen occasionally around the old house, dressed in a black silk gown with a little white lace cap. But sightings became more frequent after her burial, and her wraith was seen hurrying between the barn and the pond, apparently deeply worried. It was known that in 1745 when Bonnie Prince Charlie was marching through Lancashire Hannah feared for her money and valuables and buried them, but would never disclose where, and she died without revealing her hiding place to her relatives.

After Birchen Bower had been converted to smaller dwellings, her ghost continued to appear there, and was seen to disappear by a particular flagstone in the parlour of one of the weaver's homes. It is said that while digging a hole in the parlour floor to set up a loom, the weaver unearthed a tin box full of gold wedges which he secretly sold in Manchester, but it was many years before he divulged the secret of his sudden wealth.

However, obviously the ghost of Hannah was aware of what had happened, as she now appeared angry and threatening, and blue light seemed to flash from her eyes. Sometimes noises were heard coming from the barn, and it would glow as if on fire, but when people went there, the building was dark and silent as usual.

Eventually Birchen Bower was demolished and a factory was built on the site. Surely now the restless spirit of Hannah Beswick would be at rest and her story forgotten? And yet, they say people who have never heard of Hannah Beswick have mentioned seeing something strange – it appears to be an old lady in a black silk gown of another period, and a little lace cap!

❖

The Most Haunted House in Lancashire

C hingle Hall, built in the mid-13th century at Goosnargh, a few miles from Preston, really lives up to its reputation. As a target for ghost-hunters it has seldom disappointed its many hopeful visitors. Strange sights and sounds, cold spots, cowled figures and the touch of icy hands have all been experienced during the house's numerous changes of ownership and frequent periods of restoration and alteration.

When Adam Singleton built it around 1260, using some much older timbers, it was the first domestic building in this country to be built of brick. It is an amazing building full of surprises such as priest holes and hiding places, which came in useful during periods of religious persecution.

It was the birthplace of John Wall, who became a Franciscan priest and famous preacher, and was one of the last Catholic martyrs executed at Worcester in 1679. His head was secretly smuggled abroad as a sacred relic, but eventually came back to Chingle Hall, although its whereabouts today are unknown. It was reputed to have been hidden at the Hall, and in view of the number of possible hiding places, some of which may still not have been discovered, it seems likely that it remains there since John Wall is believed to be one of the many ghosts.

Unlike many haunted houses whose ghosts have become more elusive with the passage of time, Chingle Hall's manifestations seem to have increased in recent years when extensive restoration has exposed some of the secret rooms and passages, work which sometimes seems to reactivate ghostly phenomena. There has been a great deal of unexplained activity with pictures rattling on the walls, doors opening and slamming shut by themselves, footsteps and loud noises with no apparent cause, and visitors have felt themselves pushed unexpectedly

Chingle Hall, where many strange sights and sounds have been experienced

when they were alone in a room, or – even more alarming – have felt icy fingers clutching their own hands!

A cowled, monk-like figure has often been seen, once outside an upstairs window high above ground, and also in the room which is believed to be the birthplace of John Wall, and two hooded figures have been noticed in prayer in a room which appears to have been used as a chapel. Odd knocking noises have been heard, and dogs have been observed to behave strangely as if they are watching something unseen pass by, and problems with cameras are quite often experienced. One photographer had his camera roughly snatched away from him by invisible hands, and flung up over a beam in the ceiling!

There seems little doubt that for those with an interest in the paranormal, Chingle Hall really lives up to its reputation as Lancashire's Most Haunted House!

LEICESTERSHIRE

The Legends of Papillon Hall

On the A4304 road from Market Harborough to Lutterworth, about a mile west of Lubenham, is the site of Papillon Hall. It was erected by David Papillon in 1624, substantially altered by Sir Edwin Lutyens in 1903, and demolished in 1950.

The many strange happenings at Papillon Hall all date back to the second David Papillon, the great-great-grandson of the original builder. David the Second was a handsome man, but with a personality described as terrifyingly hypnotic and even psychic. The local population of his day was in awe of him, and called him Pamp, Old Pamp or Lord Pamp. (Papillon Hall has been known as 'Pamps' since that time.)

Pamp had the power of 'fixing' or 'setting' people. Once he came across some men who were ploughing a field in a manner that displeased him, so he 'fixed' them. They were unable to move at all until he released them at dusk. On another occasion, a footpad attempted to rob Pamp as he rode home from Market Harborough with a bag of money for wages. Pamp 'fixed' the thief, coolly left the money-bag at the man's feet, and rode home. There he stabled his horse and sent the groom back along the lane to fetch the bag. When the servant picked up the bag, the 'set' footpad was released and able to run away.

In the Lubenham area, any misfortune was attributed to Pamp's influence, and locals would attempt to evade his 'evil eye' by making the sign of the cross in their mash when making beer, or in the dough when baking bread.

The original Papillon Hall was an octagonal building with just one entrance, and stood on raised ground. The roof was in the shape of a cross, and beneath it the top storey consisted of four gabled attics. The north-east attic, always known as Pamp's attic, was bricked up by Old Pamp, leaving just a small entrance door.

Before his marriage in 1717, Pamp kept a mistress at Papillon Hall, a lady said to be of Spanish descent. She never left the Hall, but took her exercise on the leads of the roof. She died in 1715, but there is no record of her burial locally. However, when Lutyens was making major alterations to Papillon Hall in 1903, the skeleton of a woman was found in the bricked-up attic.

❖

The Spanish Shoes

B efore the Spanish lady died, she left a curse that misfortune would occur if ever her shoes left the Hall. The shoes, which still exist, actually consisted of a pair of silver and green brocade slippers fitted into a pair of pattens. The belief in this curse was so strong that whenever the house changed hands (it left the possession of the Papillons in 1764) the deeds required the new owners to keep the shoes in Papillon Hall.

This requirement has occasionally been ignored. When one owner, George Bosworth, died in 1866, the shoes were bequeathed to his daughter in Leicester. The family of the new owner, Lord Hopetoun, was disturbed by loud crashings and deafening noises from the drawing room. These continued until the shoes were obtained from George Bosworth's daughter and returned to Pamps. Only then was peace restored.

When Thomas Halford was residing at the Hall, he foolishly allowed the shoes to be taken for exhibition in Paris. The disturbances recommenced and Halford tried to get the shoes back. Unfortunately, they had to remain in Paris for the whole twelve months of the exhibition. Life at Pamps became so intolerable that the family vacated the house until the shoes were back.

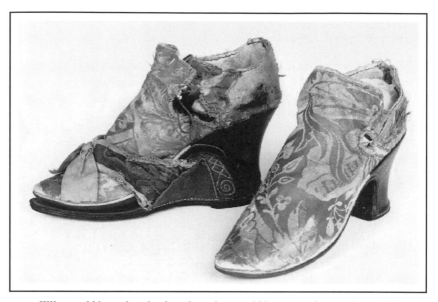

Who would have thought that these shoes could have caused so much trouble?

A later owner had a strong cupboard constructed in the wall above the main fireplace, with a padlocked metal grill for a door. The shoes were kept in this, visible but safely locked away.

When Captain Frank Bellville bought the house in 1903, he decided to have it altered and enlarged. Lutyens was engaged, and decided to add four wings to the Hall to match the name Papillon ('butterfly' in French), and to add an extra storey. It was at this time that the woman's skeleton was discovered in the attic.

Captain Bellville was not superstitious and had the shoes sent to his solicitors for safe keeping during the alterations. At Papillon Hall, all hell broke loose. Many of the builders working on the Hall suffered serious accidents, and when one of them was killed, Lutyens had to bring in a non-local firm. Captain Bellville, having sustained injuries when his pony-trap turned over, retrieved the shoes from the solicitors and kept them in the house.

Papillon Hall, after Lutyens' alterations

But in 1908, he allowed them to go to Leicester Museum. In the days that followed, Captain Bellville fractured his skull while hunting, the Hall caught fire, two servants died and three polo ponies were killed by lightning.

The shoes were fetched back to Pamps, locked behind the grill and, according to Len Beeny whose father was stud groom at the time, the key was thrown into the pond.

During the Second World War, Pamps was occupied by American servicemen of the US 82nd Airborne Division. The grill was smashed open and on at least two occasions a shoe was taken away by some of the men. Each time, the man who took the shoe was killed, and the shoe was returned to Papillon Hall. Perhaps the men were 'testing' the superstition. After the war, one shoe and patten were missing. When the Hall was demolished in 1950, the missing shoe (but not the patten) was found under the floorboards.

The shoes and the one surviving patten were put into the care of Mrs Barbara Papillon of Crowhurst Park in Sussex.

❖

The Portrait of David Papillon

A portrait of Pamp was painted in 1715, when he was 24 years of age and a bachelor. This painting has had a peculiar effect on people ever since, including many who knew nothing of the stories surrounding David Papillon. Although the Papillon family sold the house in 1764, this picture remained at Papillon Hall until 1840.

In 1800 a servant girl was woken in the night by a sound she took to be a cat. Then, by the light of the moonlight coming through the window, she saw David Papillon standing by the foot of her bed. He was dressed in a red coat and gold waistcoat, just as in his portrait. She was convinced that Pamp had emerged from the picture.

In 1840, Papillon Hall was owned by the Bosworth family but lived in by a relative, Mr Marriot. He begged Thomas Papillon to remove the portrait of his ancestor because of its sinister influence. He said that no servants would work there, because Pamp used to come out of his picture and haunt the house. Thomas agreed to help, and the picture was taken first to Acrise Place in Kent, and then to Crowhurst Park in Sussex.

From then, Pamp's ghost seems to have haunted both Papillon Hall and Crowhurst Park!

At Papillon Hall, George Atherton reports that there were many instances of unexplained crashing noises that occurred during the period in the 1930s when he was butler to Captain Bellville. Even after Papillon Hall was demolished in 1950, the owners of Papillon Farm (Mr and Mrs Hewes) claimed that their stables were haunted by Pamp.

Crowhurst Park, the new residence of Pamp's portrait, was also visited by the man in the picture. The figure of the young David Papillon was seen by people who had no previous knowledge of the history of the painting. During the early part of the 20th century, Pelham Rawstone Papillon went to live with his sister in Hastings, and Crowhurst Park was let to Colonel and Mrs Tufnell. The Tufnells were told nothing about the portrait. In 1908, Pelham was amazed to receive a letter from Mrs Tufnell imploring him to remove the picture which she said had an evil influence.

Pamp's portrait was taken to Hastings, and seems to have lost its sinister reputation since then. The young Pamp in the picture has been content to live in peace with subsequent generations of his family.

The Haunted Council House

In Leicestershire there are several haunted inns and many ghost-ridden manor houses, but this account is unique. It concerns a pre-war council house in Market Harborough, which is home to at least three ghosts.

Les Harrald was born at 19, The Broadway, and he lived there with his parents and ten brothers and sisters for 18 years. One of the ghosts that haunted the Harrald family was a young man wearing a khaki trenchcoat and a round hat. Les's mother Lorraine saw him first when she was ill in bed, and the apparition appeared on the landing. The second time she saw him, she was standing at the bottom of the stairs and watched the man glide down the stairs and then disappear.

Another person to see the ghost was Les's brother Tony, himself a soldier. He was home on leave, and was woken one night by his bed shaking. The young man in the trenchcoat was beckoning him, and Tony followed him out onto the landing. Tony was the only member of the family to see the man's face, which bore a cordite burn mark on one cheek. Tony thought the ghost was trying to tell him something, but it disappeared without doing so.

The family also heard the sound of a crying baby. This usually began each autumn as the weather grew colder. It could only be heard in one particular bedroom. The neighbours on that side of the house were pensioners, who themselves never heard the crying.

The third ghost was an old woman, seen lying on a bed by Shaun Harrald when he came in from play to fetch a coat from the wardrobe. He was terrified and rushed to find Les, who was downstairs watching television. By this time, however, the apparition was gone. Anne Harrald saw this woman too, at 5.30 one morning, going from one bedroom to another.

The one experience that Les himself had occurred when he woke to find his bed shaking. Assuming that it was one of his brothers or sister playing a trick, he looked underneath his bed but no one was there. His sister Lindsey entered the room, and Les told her to watch his bed because it would shake by itself. Lindsey rushed him downstairs to his parents, but Les remembers catching a brief glimpse of an eerie light shining from the wall, as he was rushed from the room.

The Harrald family told few people about their ghosts, as they thought they would not be believed. They left the house in 1974, and the next tenants were a Roman Catholic family, the Butlers.

They were more alarmed by the disturbances. Seven year old Richard saw a little old lady with a lantern who tried to tuck him into bed one night. When he called out, she faded away. On other occasions, Mrs Jean Butler heard her name called, and heard a noise she described as 'like a baby crawling along the floor'. The happenings continued until the summer of 1978, when the Butlers moved out for two months while modernisation work was carried out.

While work was in progress, the builders too began to experience strange phenomena. One man felt someone touch his back, and caught a glimpse of a hand on his shoulder. The shock caused him to fall downstairs and break his leg. It was at this stage that the story got into the local press.

When the Butler family moved back in, the happenings grew more frequent, and Jean Butler consulted the parish priest, Father Marian. He told her that it was dangerous to try to exorcise ghosts but also wrong to try to make contact with them. He advised the family to put up a rosary and leave a bible open in the house. Jean bought two rosaries, hanging one in the kitchen and the other in the bedroom. She kept six bibles in the house, two of them permanently open at the 23rd Psalm, as she felt this might ward off evil spirits. The Butlers moved out of the house a few years later. The house remained empty for a while, many prospective tenants refusing to move in because of the house's reputation.

When Graham Bullivant and his family took the tenancy in 1983, someone had hung bunches of garlic all over the house. He promptly threw them out. 'I do like garlic,' he told me, 'but not in that quantity!' He was not bothered by the history of the house, but admitted that one or two odd things have occurred.

Graham's wife sometimes felt that she was not alone in an upstairs room, when in fact she was. One Sunday morning, their son said that he'd been talking to a man in the house, when Graham knew that there was only the two of them present.

At 8.30 one evening, his wife was out and the children were in bed. Graham was sitting, drinking a cup of coffee, when his two dogs got up and stood growling. A strange clicking noise came from the kitchen. On investigating, he found that every cupboard door had come open; what he had heard was the magnetic catches opening. Fortunately, Graham found these events strange but in no way intimidating.

LINCOLNSHIRE

Scrimshaw's Poltergeist

In 1909 Joe Scrimshaw, a fruit farmer, had a new house built on the old Turnover Bank, which soon became known as 'The Haunted House'.

Sometime between moving in and the start of the haunting, which was on 12th February 1923, his wife had left him, taking one of their two children with her. The other, Olive, who was 14 years old when the happening occurred, lived with Skrimmie and his mother who received help from a daily woman named Harriet Ward.

Strange things happened in the late afternoon when Granny Scrimshaw tried without success to light the oil lamps and had to send Olive out to borrow candles from a neighbour. They too refused to be lit, neither would they flare for Joe who ate his supper in a bad mood.

Suddenly, in the half light of the sitting room fire which was struggling to keep alight, the family's pianola, which was estimated to weigh some five hundredweight, slid by itself from its place against the wall and moved about the room, then toppled in a jangling heap on the floor.

This was followed by the pictures dropping one by one from the wall, ornaments falling from the mantelpiece and the heavy dining table scuttling about like the pianola. Worse was to come when the barometer, Joe's most valued possession, leaped down onto the floor to join the picture glass and figurines.

Then crashing came from the kitchen and so, to avoid more damage, the crockery was stacked neatly on the large table instead of being balanced in the china pantry. The door was locked and a few minutes later everything was dashed to smithereens on the floor. Nothing was chipped or cracked in two, everything was reduced to shards.

Neighbours were called in and witnessed the mayhem and after a night of further uproar Olive was sent to lodge with relatives in Norfolk and never returned to live in her father's house.

Word soon got out that Skrimmie had a poltergeist and this attracted the local and national press plus lots of sightseers who got the rough edge of Joe's sharp tongue. He also received a lot of letters which included one from Sir Arthur Conan Doyle who thought his teenage daughter could have encouraged the poltergeist. He suggested amongst other things that the house should be well ventilated, but the troubles remained even with fresh air and Olive's absence.

The local vicar was not interested in Joe's predicament, but a farmer from neighbouring Wisbech St Mary was. He suggested that perhaps he had not got a poltergeist, maybe someone had cast the Evil Eye upon him. He suggested that Harriet Mary Holmes, the local wise-woman cum smallholder, of Chalk Road, might be able to exorcise the place and I am told the *News of the World* paid her fee. She went to the lonely house on Turnover Bank where she performed her traditional spell-breaking, using a small medicine bottle filled with a number of black-headed apple pips, some pins, a paring from Joe's fingernail and pieces of hair taken from his mother and daughter. The bottle was well stoppered and placed in the hot coals of the kitchen range, then she locked the door and would not let the Scrimshaws in until the bottle had burst from the heat of the fire, taking the hex with it.

The spell-breaker was quite commonplace, using intimate links with the possessed and the malevolence, but did it really work or was 'it', albeit the Evil Eye or the poltergeist, more clever than the wise-woman? For on 6th March Mrs Holmes was found face down, drowned in some six inches of dyke water. Everybody agreed that the old lady, who was in robust health and knew the area like the back of her hand, had no business being in the dyke.

She lies in Gorefield churchyard beside her husband John, but the strange thing is that just about the time of her death Joe Scrimshaw reckoned all hell broke loose in his house for just a few minutes, then 'it' went away. Although he was never again aware of the presence, others have been and are!

❖

The Haunting of Epworth Rectory

T he Rev Samuel Wesley and his large family lived in the Rectory at Epworth, which he had built in 1709 after a fire destroyed the original house on the site. So it was quite a new building with no ghostly history in December 1716 when a strange entity that they christened 'Old Jeffrey' unexpectedly arrived. According to Samuel's son, John Wesley, later the founder of Methodism, it was about ten o'clock at night on 2nd December 1716 that a servant, Robert Brown, heard a knock and what sounded like a groan. He opened the door, but found no one outside, and this happened twice more, which seemed strange. Then when he and the other servants went upstairs to bed, at the top of the stairs they found a handmill turning by itself, and during the night there was a weird, inexplicable sound like a turkey gobbling, and other noises as if someone had stumbled.

The next day while one of the maids was in the dairy she heard knocking on a dairy shelf which seemed to have no apparent cause and so frightened her that she screamed and dropped a tray of butter.

Next evening one of the Wesley daughters was in the dining room when she heard the rustling of a silk dress as if someone was walking about in the room although she was alone there. Later as she was telling her sister about it there was knocking from underneath the table, and the door latch rattled up and down.

Odd noises continued such as heavy footsteps on the stairs, and when Mrs Wesley, who was inclined to dismiss it all as imagination, went into the nursery she heard the sound of a cradle rocking, although there was no cradle there.

Epworth Old Rectory, where the Wesley children encountered 'Old Jeffrey'

Samuel Wesley, too, had heard nothing himself and had no time for such nonsense, but during family prayers there was an absolute cacophony of knocking all round the room, and later he found that when he tapped his walking stick on the floor, more taps answered him. Called 'Old Jeffrey' by the family, because apparently someone of this name had died in the house previously, their noisy poltergeist kept up a succession of noises, day and night, which the children found highly entertaining. Far from being frightened, they loved to chase from room to room following the sounds, but their huge mastiff dog would tremble and hide himself when Old Jeffrey was in action.

Mr Wesley kept a diary of events, recording how he was 'thrice pushed by an invisible power'. One night when there was a noise as if several people were walking about overhead and then running up and downstairs, Mr and Mrs Wesley thought the children would be frightened, so went down together and were startled by a clatter as if someone had emptied a bag of money at their feet, followed by a noise as if lots of bottles had been smashed to pieces. The phenomena consisted mostly of noises of every kind, but one day 19 year old Hetty fled when she saw what seemed to be a man in a loose nightgown coming down the stairs towards her. A small creature was glimpsed one day, which Mrs Wesley described as a headless badger and one of the servants thought was like a white rabbit.

Although friends advised the family to leave the house, Mr Wesley stoutly refused, saying he would not fly from the Devil. And indeed, by January 1717 the house had resumed its customary peaceful atmosphere and Old Jeffrey, or whatever noisy spirit had briefly taken up its abode there, had apparently departed elsewhere.

Epworth Rectory is now a museum open to the public from March to October, and a target for enthusiastic ghost-hunters who sometimes spend the night there. Apparently odd unexplained noises have been heard from time to time, but after more than 300 years it seems safe to assume that the Rectory has seen the last of its noisy poltergeist.

MIDDLESEX

The Ghost of the London Tube

I f you happen to be at Covent Garden Underground Station late one night, and some tall, distinguished looking stranger suddenly disappears before your very eyes, don't think you are imagining things. You've probably seen William Terris, a ghost who has been quite a regular commuter there.

At least, that's what Jack Hayden, once a travelling ticket inspector there, told me when we talked about the dozens of times he encountered the ghost he called Billy.

'The first few times I was terrified in case I met him again,' said Jack. 'Whenever I was working late at Covent Garden I used to expect him, as he always came at about the same time. But after a while, I began to feel very friendly towards him. I did try to talk to him when I saw him, but although he made gestures with his hands, he never spoke to me.'

Mr Hayden told me that he could always sense when the ghost was around. He noticed that there was something different about the atmosphere, a disturbing chill unlike the warm gusts of air one usually finds on most underground stations.

'He'd let me know he was there,' said Jack, who often used to work late in the underground mess room. 'He'd give a gentle little rattle at the door, and often it would open slightly. Sometimes I've looked out, and he'd be standing there outside, leaning against the wall. Then he'd walk away down the emergency stairs.'

I wondered what he looked like, this lonely phantom.

'He looks absolutely real,' Jack told me, describing a tall, handsome man wearing a grey suit of Victorian style, a homburg hat and white

William Terriss, one of the great Victorian theatre idols, now a regular commuter

gloves. 'The first time I saw him I thought by the way he was dressed that he'd come from the opera house.'

Jack Hayden's first encounter with the ghost was in the late Fifties. 'I had been working at Covent Garden for three or four years before I saw him,' he told me. 'I'll always remember it, he appeared to me on Christmas Eve.'

Jack was working late in the mess room when he heard the door handle rattle. He looked out, and there was a man in an old-fashioned suit.

'I thought he'd lost his way, and tried to direct him to the lift, or down the stairs, but he turned away, and all of a sudden he'd disappeared. I didn't know what to think, then three days afterwards I was working late at the station again when I heard this yell outside. We had a West Indian chap working as a porter, and he came rushing into the room, and fainted! After he came round he said "I saw a ghost looking in through the door at you." He described what he'd seen and it was exactly the same man I'd seen myself.'

After this, Jack Hayden reported the strange happenings to Head Office, and later it was arranged for a medium to visit the station. 'He went into a trance straight away,' said Jack, 'I'd never seen anything like that before. The ghost was actually talking through him. He told us who he was, and how he had been murdered, and now was earthbound and couldn't find rest. This was the first suspicion we had that it was the ghost of William Terriss. Later on there was another séance at the station, and other people spoke to him and tried to help him.'

So who was William Terriss and why should his ghost still linger in the neighbourhood of Covent Garden?

Handsome William Terriss was one of the best loved actors of his day, and a string of successful melodramas at the Adelphi Theatre had made him the darling of the Victorian theatre-going public. But his popularity was to lead to an untimely death through another man's insane jealousy.

Richard Prince was a minor actor in the same company, but he had convinced himself that but for Terriss, he too could be a star. He brooded on his imaginary wrongs, and when the management told him that he was no longer needed at the Adelphi, he rushed into Terriss's dressing room full of angry accusations.

Terriss, genuinely sorry to know that Prince had lost his job, tried to offer friendly encouragement, and gave him some money, but Prince, now quite unbalanced, was bent on a murderous plan.

William Terriss always used a private entrance to the theatre instead of the stage door. It was in Bull Inn Court, and on the night of the 16th December 1897, when he walked down this dark alley with a friend, Prince was waiting, his hand clutching a butcher's knife that he had bought with the money Terriss had given him.

As Terriss put his key in the door, Prince flung himself upon him, and before his horrified friend could intervene, the actor had collapsed, stabbed to the heart.

Carried into the theatre, he died in the arms of his son-in-law, the actor Seymour Hicks, surrounded by his company, while his adoring public, ignorant of the tragedy, waited for the curtain to rise on another of Breezy Bill's successes.

But it was not the last that people would see or hear of William Terriss. It had been his habit to tap a lighthearted tattoo on dressing room doors with his walking stick when he arrived for a performance, and soon after his death odd rapping noises were heard in his old dressing room and sometimes unexplained footsteps and the sensation of an unseen presence were experienced backstage.

Then in 1928 an actress was resting in her dressing room, which happened to be the one used by Jessie Millward, Terriss's leading lady at the time of his murder. She was just falling asleep when her chaise longue began to vibrate beneath her, then to rock violently as if it was being kicked from underneath. On another occasion she saw a strange greenish light hovering by her mirror, and there were often unexplained knocks on the door when no one was there.

A figure resembling Terriss has been seen near Bull Inn Court, and of course, he has been no stranger to Covent Garden tube for years. Poor William Terriss, once the idol of the Victorian public, whose tragic murder seems to have doomed him to haunt the neighbourhood he knew so well. When will he take his last curtain call?

❖

A Screaming Queen and Other Hampton Court Ghosts

I n the summer of 2000, the famous ghosts of Hampton Court were subjected to all the latest ghost-detecting equipment, including £50,000 thermal imaging cameras. Apparently two women on separate guided tours had fainted at the same spot in the Haunted Gallery after becoming icy cold, and feeling as if they had been punched, and it was decided to call in ghostbuster Dr Richard Wiseman and his team to investigate some of Hampton Court's famous phenomena.

For his fifth wife Henry VIII chose Catherine Howard, a pretty, vivacious young girl, his rose without a thorn, but unknown to the King, Catherine had a promiscuous past, and soon after her marriage to her ageing, gouty husband, she embarked upon an indiscreet affair with Thomas Culpeper, a youth of Henry's bedchamber. Their secret meetings were no secret to some of the Palace staff. And although Henry was the last to know, when he did unwillingly accept the truth about his youthful wife, her fate was sealed.

Catherine was confined to her rooms at Hampton Court, and the story goes that while imprisoned she escaped from her guards and ran down the long gallery to the entrance to the Royal Chapel, to

Catherine Howard, said to have been both seen and heard at Hampton Court

make an anguished appeal for forgiveness to Henry, who was attending service there. But she was captured and dragged away screaming, and for centuries Catherine's ghost in a white gown is reputed to have been seen and heard in what is now known as the Haunted Gallery.

Did this emotionally powerful event somehow become imprinted on its surroundings? There are numerous accounts of sightings, or the sound of agonised screaming, and many people have reported sensations of extreme coldness, and feelings of despair and acute misery in the region of the entrance to the Chapel.

Dr Wiseman and his team conducted night-time vigils using thermal imaging cameras and other high-tech equipment, and also talked to many visitors to the Palace.

So did the wraith of Henry's unfortunate Queen make a personal appearance? Apparently nothing so exciting happened, but about 50% of visitors questioned reported having unusual experiences in the gallery such as a sense of presence, a sudden drop in temperature, dizziness or sickness.

Jane Seymour, who has been seen leaving the Queen's Apartments, holding a lighted taper

Dr Wiseman and his colleagues thought that feelings of unusually cold air could be explained by draughts from the gallery's many concealed doors, but they were surprised at the number of responses received from visitors. At one stage the thermal cameras detected what appeared to be a supernatural figure in the gallery, but when it was seen to open a cupboard and take out a vacuum cleaner, they realised that Catherine Howard it wasn't.

Yet another of Henry's wives is said to haunt Hampton Court. Jane Seymour, his third wife, who died after giving birth to his only legitimate son, Edward, has been seen – a white clad figure, leaving the Queen's Apartments and wandering round the Silver Stick Gallery, holding a lighted taper, then continuing downstairs to Clock Court.

Grace-and-favour residents living in the south wing in 1829 noticed what sounded like a whirring noise, and a woman's voice coming from behind a wall, and others reported seeing the apparition of a woman in a long grey hooded robe. Workmen were called to make a hole in the wall, which revealed a sealed-off room containing a 16th century spinning wheel!

It was about that time that Hampton church was demolished, and the tomb of Mistress Sibell Penn, nurse to Edward VI, was disturbed. She was well known for her spinning, and it was thought that the upheaval at the church had brought her back to the wheel, and to make occasional appearances. The ghost was recognisable as Mistress Penn, as it closely resembled the stone effigy on her tomb.

In the late 1800s, Princess Frederica of Hanover was living at Hampton Court, where she gave birth to a baby, Victoria, in March 1881. One night she was startled to wake up and see an unknown old woman bending over the cradle. The figure vanished, and it was thought it resembled Mistress Sibell Penn, not apparently a good omen as the baby died soon afterwards.

Another resident about a hundred years ago complained of noises in the night coming from Fountain Court, but nothing was done until workmen had to lay new drains there, and the remains of two Civil War Cavaliers were discovered in a shallow grave. And after they had been properly buried, there were no more unexplained sounds in the night.

NORFOLK

The Brown Lady of Raynham Hall

I n the realm of stately home hauntings the Brown Lady of Raynham Hall is rightly one of the most famous, with a host of dramatic sightings since her death in 1726.

She is believed to be Dorothy Walpole, sister of Britain's first Prime Minister, Robert Walpole of Houghton Hall, and although those who have encountered her ghost describe its appearance as frightening and even 'malevolent', in life she was a beautiful and charming woman, but whose fondness for pretty clothes verged on the extravagant. This may have led to her serious differences with her husband, the 2nd Marquess Townshend, known as 'Turnip' Townshend, who introduced the vegetable to England and revolutionised crop rotation.

There are different versions of Dorothy's story. Her grandfather was made guardian of Charles Townshend, then 13 years old, and when in due course Dorothy was 15, and Charles 12 years older, he fell deeply in love and wanted to marry her. But Dorothy's father refused to allow it, as he thought he would be accused of having his eye on the Townshend fortune and property.

One version of the story says Dorothy did not share Charles's feelings, in fact she found him repulsive. But the more romantic version has her plunging into a frivolous life of parties and scandalous behaviour to forget her broken heart, ultimately becoming the mistress of a well-known roué, Lord Wharton.

Meanwhile, Charles Townshend had married, but his wife died in 1713, and he and Dorothy were united at last. There seems little doubt that after a time the marriage was unhappy, and whatever caused Charles's change of heart towards her, he deprived Dorothy of the care of

The Brown Lady of Raynham Hall, as seen by Country Life *photographers in the 1930s*

her children who were put in charge of his mother. Miserable without them and unkindly treated by her husband, Dorothy is said to have been confined to her rooms, at Raynham Hall, and within a short time died at the age of 40.

One tradition says that Dorothy was starved to death, and another that she fell, or was pushed, down the grand staircase and was killed. But the contemporary announcement of her death, on 29th March 1726, gives the cause as smallpox.

Many hauntings have a tragic background, and whatever the truth about the manner of Dolly Townshend's death, she did not rest in peace and her ghost was soon seen by servants, family and visitors.

One important visitor was George IV, when Prince Regent, who was, of course, put in the State Bedroom – with unfortunate results. He roused the whole household, reporting furiously that he had been disturbed by 'a little lady all dressed in brown, with dishevelled hair and a face of ashy paleness', who stood by his bedside. 'I will not pass another hour in this accursed house,' cried his Highness, 'for I have seen that what I hope to God I may never see again.'

The Brown Lady's sighting in 1849 was reported in *Rifts in the Veil* by Lucia Stone, a member of a large houseparty at Raynham. Major Loftus, a relative of the hosts Lord and Lady Charles Townshend, had stayed up late with another guest playing chess, and as they went up to bed, his attention was called to a lady in a brown dress standing on the landing. He did not recognise her as one of the guests, but when he went to speak to her, she vanished.

Determined to waylay the mysterious lady, he waited up the following night, and managed to come face to face with her. In the light of his lamp he could see her clearly and described her wearing a richly brocaded brown dress with a coif on her head, but to his horror instead of eyes she had two dark, hollow sockets. He made a sketch of what he had seen and showed it next morning to the other guests, which inspired some of them to do some ghost-hunting on their own account, but the Brown Lady was not tempted to make another appearance.

But the effect on the servants was unfortunate; the entire staff gave notice and left! Although Lord Charles declared that he had seen the family ghost several times, he was suspicious that this time some annoying practical joker might be responsible, and in lieu of the missing staff, he brought in a number of police, but no trickster or the Brown Lady herself rewarded their vigil.

The ghost received an unexpected reception when Captain Marryat, the famous author of *Mr Midshipman Easy*, was staying at Raynham Hall. The Captain briskly dismissed the notion of ghosts and insisted on sleeping in the haunted bedroom, which contained a portrait of the Brown Lady. A lesser man might have felt uneasy as in the flickering candlelight the eyes in the picture appeared unnaturally alive, and the expression on the face seemed the embodiment of evil. But not Marryat; he was getting ready for bed when two other guests arrived at his room to ask his advice about a gun for the shooting party next day.

Captain Marryat went with them to see the gun and was returning along the shadowy corridor when he saw a woman coming towards him. Her feet made no sound, and the lamp she was holding illuminated a figure unmistakably the image of the portrait in his room. According to Marryat, the apparition looked at him 'in such a diabolical manner' that even he was frightened and, gun in hand, he fired point-blank, full in her face. The bullets went straight though her and lodged in the door behind, and the figure vanished.

It's said that the brave Captain slept with his loaded pistols under his pillow for the rest of his visit.

Gwladys, Marchioness Townshend, in *True Ghost Stories* (1936), says that her son George and a friend, when they were small boys, met a lady on the staircase, who frightened and puzzled them because they could see the stairs through her!

And in the 1920s Sir Henry ('Tim') Birkin sat up one night hoping to encounter the Brown Lady, but although he waited in vain, his dog showed signs of acute terror in the small hours.

Marchioness Townshend also mentions other spectres at Raynham such as two ghost children, a phantom spaniel whose paws patter on the staircase although he is not seen, and the charming Red Cavalier. This is the Duke of Monmouth, Charles II's ill-fated son, who once stayed at

Raynham Hall with his royal father. He haunts the bedroom he once used, now known as the Monmouth Room, and the Marchioness tells the story of a lovely 'deb of the year' who insisted on sleeping there, hoping for a visit from the notorious charmer.

But despite the Duke's well-known eye for a pretty woman, she was unlucky. The next occupant of the room a few days later was a 'spinster of uncertain age' who, according to her hostess, was sadly destined to live a drab life devoid of romance. However, she woke that night to find the dashing Red Cavalier standing at the end of her bed, 'smiling in a most encouraging manner'. As he went he gave her a charming courtly bow and faded away through the wall, leaving her with a cherished memory of her glamorous visitor.

The famous photograph of the Brown Lady has been frequently reproduced in books about ghosts and hauntings. It happened in the Thirties that two photographers from *Country Life* magazine were taking a series of photographs of Raynham Hall. Captain Provand was photographing the staircase when his assistant, Indra Shira, suddenly noticed a misty figure approaching down the stairs. He quickly urged Captain Provand to take an exposure, which he did, although he himself had seen nothing. He protested that Indra Shira must have imagined it, and declared that even if there was something there, nothing would appear when the negative was developed.

But Indra Shira insisted he had seen a figure so ethereal that the steps were visible through it, and later when they were developing the negatives the Captain could see that there was definitely something on the staircase negative. Indra Shira hurried downstairs to the chemist below their studio and brought Benjamin Jones back to be a witness that the negative had not been tampered with. Later a number of experts examined it and were satisfied that the picture had not been faked in any way.

There seems no doubt that Raynham Hall is haunted by echoes of its past. In *True Ghost Stories* the Marchioness Townshend says that at times the sound of whispers and the swish of silken skirts testify 'that the picture gallery is alive with the "Quality" who ruffled it in the days when the splendour of the Great House was undiminished'. And sometimes in one room the heavy chairs which are usually set against the walls are found in the morning companionably grouped around a large card table! Are the Brown Lady and the Red Cavalier among the players I wonder?

❖

Bircham Newton

There were many airfields throughout East Anglia during the Second World War from which the RAF and USAAF bombers and fighter planes flew the Channel on their dangerous missions, and perhaps it is not surprising that so much courage and cameraderie coupled with tragedy and loss has left more than memories.

Many of these former wartime airfields have a history of strange happenings – the sound of a plane in an empty sky, a man in uniform who casually walks through a solid wall, or who hitches a lift, only to vanish en route.

Perhaps the best known of these airfields is Bircham Newton, originally built in 1914 and now home to the National Construction College. In 1970 a film crew were there making a management training film and, while they were working, without warning a heavy studio lamp suddenly fell towards Peter Clark, one of the crew, who was standing directly underneath. Luckily for him, just as it was about to hit him it swerved away, just as if it had been diverted by an unseen hand! No one apparently thought much of this at the time, but even stranger things were to follow.

Later, Kevin Garry, another member of the crew, discovered that there were two squash courts at Bircham, and he borrowed a racquet and ball to play, but none of the others wanted to join him so off he went, having picked up the only key to the building. At first he practised in the left hand court, and then he tried the right hand one, and while he was playing he heard footsteps coming along the viewing gallery behind him. He simply assumed that one of the crew had decided to join him after all, then remembered that the door was locked and he had the key. At that moment he heard a sigh which made the hairs on the back of his neck prickle, and when he looked round, there in the gallery watching him was a man in RAF uniform. And as he looked, the figure vanished! Kevin wasted no more time – he fled.

When Peter Clark heard what had happened he suggested they take a tape recorder to the courts to see if it recorded anything. 'It was a warm moonlit night when we returned to the courts,' said Peter. 'We visited the left hand court which felt completely normal, but when we went into the court on the right the atmosphere was so cold, so frightening that it was like stepping into another world.'

The two men left the tape running and waited outside. They had locked the door, and were able to see that no one else got into the building. As they collected the tape just as it was coming to an end, they heard footsteps coming along the gallery. They came nearer but there was no one to be seen, and the frightened men grabbed the recorder and ran.

Many people, including myself, have heard this tape which sounds as if it comes from a large, echoing building, perhaps a hangar. There are metallic sounds, muffled speech and a woman's voice, but what she is saying is impossible to identify. The sound of a piston-engined aircraft can be heard, and finally there is a really strange loud noise. The tape used was brand new, so there was no question of previous recordings being on it, and exterior sounds could not have penetrated the nine inch brick walls of the courts. In any case, it was near midnight on a calm, quiet night.

Later Peter Clark returned to the airfield with a medium, who as soon as he entered the squash courts made contact with a dead airman. On the tape the medium can be heard asking, 'What is your name?' And finally the answer came – 'Wiley'. Clark discovered in local newspaper files that an airman called Wiley had committed suicide at the airfield in World War Two.

Enquiries revealed that the airfield had had a reputation for being haunted for a long time. A student on a construction course had his bedclothes pulled off at night by an unseen hand, another found his curtains torn down and thrown across the room, radiators in the officers' mess were always being turned off, and one student left hurriedly after seeing a figure in RAF uniform walk straight through a solid wall. Some of the recordings were broadcast on the BBC and several listeners who had been stationed at Bircham Newton during the last war wrote in to say that it was common knowledge that the ghost of an airman was frequently seen about the place. It was also considered to be an unlucky airfield. In the early part of the war after the American Air Force moved in, on one occasion they despatched 13 bombers on a raid from which not one returned.

A BBC TV team invited two leading spiritualists to the airfield, taking care not to tell them anything about previous happenings. They both immediately sensed the spirit of a dead airman in the squash courts, and the famous medium John Sutton commented that there was a lot of psychic power being generated in the building.

John Sutton went into a trance and began to speak in a sort of hoarse whisper, the voice of an airman called Dusty Miller, who had been killed in a crash with his friends Pat Sullivan and Gerry Arnold when their plane came down in flames behind a church. When Sutton came out of his trance he said that the three airmen had been keen squash players and had made a pact that if anything happened to them they would try to meet again in the building.

'Very often people don't realise what has happened when they die,' he said. 'Their sense of time is quite different and these three airmen were earthbound because they didn't realise they were dead. They desperately needed help.' He had told them that they must let go of the earth, look up and go towards the light.

Later, records were checked and it was found that an RAF Anson plane had crashed behind Bircham church killing the crew of three.

By coincidence, the BBC sent a woman reporter, Rita Dando, to Bircham Newton, and she arrived with a woman friend later the same day. They borrowed the key to the squash courts and locked themselves in, but the locked door flew open and then slammed shut three times. They knew there was no one else in the building and they had the only key. Then their tape recorder refused to function, so they returned to their hotel where they found the tape recorder was now working perfectly.

So are the ghostly happenings at Bircham Newton all in the past? In 1999 a film crew were at the airfield making a television film for a Japanese TV programme whose viewers are apparently fascinated by the paranormal. They found the atmosphere in the squash courts unnaturally icy, and although there was no breeze, the door slammed suddenly.

But despite no ghost taking part in their programme, the Anglia Society for Paranormal Research, who have been visiting the airfield regularly for at least ten years, were able to supply evidence that Bircham Newton's haunting reputation is well earned. 'The place is very haunted, not just the squash court but two or three other buildings,' Keith Webster, the Society's technical co-ordinator, told me.

They have come to the conclusion that the entities which haunt the squash court are two men and a woman and have based this on the voices heard. They leave their micro-transmitter on the wall inside while they remain outside with their tape recorder, and it is only afterwards when they play back the tape that they can hear the voices interacting with their own. Sometimes they have heard the ghosts taking their transmitter apart and reassembling it, and once they heard the woman's voice say 'Pack it in you two'. They know that the entities are aware of their presence as they have actually heard them refer to his fellow member Wendy Hudson by name!

They have formed the opinion that when the plane crashed killing the three airmen who haunted the squash court, there was an unauthorised WRAF Officer on the plane, probably the girlfriend of one of the men.

The group from the Anglia Society for Paranormal Research have taken photographs which show swirling mist like a vortex but another shows shapes which can be discerned as those of a man and a woman together, and Keith Webster thinks that the squash courts may have been used for a romantic rendezvous.

Recordings have also produced loud noises and knocking, footsteps and whistling and occasionally voices. Are some of these sounds some kind of playback from those wartime days so long ago?

The ghosts in the squash courts seem more like actual entities but, I wondered, are they always there, earthbound, or do they come and go? Keith Webster said he thinks they come and go. 'We see strange lights sometimes like a beam or a spotlight which could possibly be the entrance to a parallel universe.'

Someone who served as a WAAF at the airfield during the last war recalled that often fellow WAAFs on night duty reported hearing a car race along and crash into the wall of a hangar, but when they rushed out to help the driver, there was nothing to be seen. Another story relates to a phantom sports car full of laughing airmen which races across the base to crash into the back of a hangar. Surely it must be the same one? Sixty years later, are the ghosts of those brave airmen still living their war? Still forgetting tomorrow's rendezvous with danger in a night out with their mates, or a romantic liaison with a lover? The medium John Sutton told the three in the squash court to leave the earth behind and go towards the light. Let's hope some day this will happen.

NORTHAMPTONSHIRE

The Phantom Army

Grafton Regis is built on a hill, nine miles from Northampton. It is a tranquil place now, but royal romance, intrigue and passion are all threads running through the history of this small village. Here in the forest nearby Edward IV met his future wife, the young widow Elizabeth Gray, eldest daughter of the Woodville family who owned the manor house at Grafton. Several years later, lusty Henry VIII brought his mistress Anne Boleyn to the manor house. He was besotted with Anne and was desperately petitioning the Pope for a divorce from his first wife Catherine of Aragon. The last interview between the King and Cardinals Wolsey and Campeggio, took place at the royal residence at Grafton.

Events in history once more touched the quiet village in the Civil War, when in December 1643 the manor house was besieged by the Parliamentarian army. Both Grafton and Towcester were held by the Royalists and this was preventing the passage of ammunition from Northampton to Gloucester. Sergeant Major Skippon, in charge of a body of Parliamentarian troops, joined a detachment of soldiers from Northampton and set off to the manor house at Grafton Regis. On Thursday night, 21st December, 1,000 Roundhead troops marched into Grafton from Lathbury, six miles away. They met with fierce opposition from the Royalists, and it was not until Sunday night, which was Christmas Eve, that Sir John Digby surrendered the house to the Parliamentarians. On Christmas morning, Philip Skippon gave orders to his men to set fire to the huts they had built in the field, and, to prevent further opposition, also to fire the manor house. He thanked God for the few casualties, and released the women, children and innocent parties. This done, the Parliamentarians set off to Newport Pagnell, with their prisoners.

The activities of the ghostly army continued for an hour or more

Three centuries later, on the night of 21st December 1943, the streets of Grafton Regis were silent and dark. The blackout was complete, not a chink of light escaping from the darkened windows. In a field not far from the village, six Irish farm labourers, four O'Donnell brothers and two mates, were spending another cramped and cold night in a caravan. With most able bodied men serving in the forces, vital land work was carried out by older men assisted by prisoners of war, displaced

Europeans, land army girls and men from neutral Ireland. Far from home and their loved ones, the six men must have felt very isolated, especially at Christmas time.

After settling down for the night the Irishmen were awakened in the early hours of the morning by the sounds of horses galloping and men shouting. It seemed to them as if cavalry regiments were fighting outside, with horses' hooves thudding and harnesses creaking and jingling. A baleful light shone through the small windows of the caravan, and the men got out of their beds to find out what was going on. They could see nothing, but the threatening noises increased, with the yells of men, the muffled roar of cannon, the blast of trumpets and the beat of drums. The activities of the ghostly army carried on for an hour or more and then the noises died away. The Irishmen were too scared to go outside, so they remained huddled together to await the dawn.

The next morning, the supervisor, who was based at Northampton, set off in his van with the weekly wage packets of farm labourers working in the Roade area. He arrived in Grafton Regis at about 9.30 am, and went to the field adjacent to the farm buildings where the Irishmen should have been working. There was no sign of them, and when the farmer said he had not seen them that morning, the supervisor became concerned and drove to the caravan. Inside, he found six very frightened men who were immensely relieved to see him. They explained about their unnerving experience of the previous night. Their tale was met with a good deal of scepticism by the supervisor who privately thought that the men had overslept after a heavy drinking bout at the White Hart! But it took a lot of persuasion on his part to get them back to work, and then only on the condition that their caravan was moved to another site.

What the Irishmen could not have known was that it was 300 years to the day that a battle had taken place in Grafton Regis. As past momentous events are believed by some to leave an indelible impression, was the ghostly army that they heard as they huddled together terrified in their caravan, a re-enactment of the storming of the manor house by the Roundheads?

The Restless Ghost

Hannington is a small, quiet village situated between Northampton and Kettering, with a ghost story dating back to the 15th century. On New Year's Eve in 1425, a local farmer called William Pell was returning from Kettering market when he was set upon by robbers. He was brutally murdered, stripped of his clothes and valuables, then buried in an orchard near his farm.

In 1675 Richard Clarke, a maltster, moved into the old Pell farmhouse with his wife and two young sons. After living there for a short time, the family began to be disturbed by many strange incidents which frightened and alarmed them. In the middle of the night, doors which had been locked were unbolted and flung off their hinges. Windows were broken, loud bangs and knockings vibrated through the house. Everyone became on edge after so many sleepless nights, and the maltster's wife begged her husband to move out before one of them was harmed. Reluctantly he agreed, although he said first he would have a word with some of the neighbours. They told him that the house did not have the reputation of being haunted, but Richard Clarke decided that by spring, if matters had not improved, they would move out.

The weather turned bitterly cold and by the end of December, snow began to fall heavily. On New Year's Eve, Clarke had to go into one of the outbuildings to turn his malt. He was carrying a lantern and the night was dark and windy, with snowflakes swirling about his face as he came out of the barn, when something moved in the corner of the yard. Clarke swung his lantern high to shed some light on the shadows. What he saw made him shout out in fear, 'What the devil are you doing here?' For the figure of a man was standing in the dark corner, dressed in strange clothes. He was wearing a long serge coast with full sleeves, light breeches fastened at the knees and a high crowned hat with a wide brim. The man, about 40 years of age, had a small, pointed beard. As there was no answer from the stranger the maltster's unease deepened but, before he could gain the safety of his back door, the silent figure appeared in front of him and held up his hand, bidding him to go no further and demanding to speak with him. He declared himself to be the spirit of a person long since dead, murdered near the farmhouse, 250 years before. The apparition told him that in his former life he had been William Pell, a farmer, and had lived in the house that Clarke now occupied. After Richard recovered from the shock, he managed to ask Pell why he was roaming the earth after so many years. The ghost explained that he had wandered as a spirit soon after his murder, but a local friar had found him and exorcised him for a period of 250 years. Now that time had elapsed and he was again free to wander until he could find someone willing to carry out his wishes. Pell explained that he had been killed before he could tell his wife and children where he had hidden his documents and money; if Richard would go to this secret place, find the hoard, and distribute it amongst his descendants, he could then rest in peace. The apparition asked Clarke to go to Southwark Bridge in London the next day, for his money was buried in a nearby house which he had once owned.

By this time the maltster was shivering with cold and fright and would have promised to go anywhere to get away from the ghost of Pell. He told him that he could not go for a fortnight as he had some business to attend to, but in fact he had no intention of going at all. The spirit disappeared and Clarke was able to go into his house and thankfully shut the door. Over the next few days the distrustful ghost visited Clarke three times and reminded him of his promise. Unable to stand it any longer, the maltster went to see the rector, who advised him to carry out the spirit's wishes and also suggested, oddly, that he should on no account eat or drink at the house where Pell would lead him.

Eventually on 7th January 1676 Clarke set off to London where the ghost was to meet him on Southwark Bridge. There Pell led him to a nearby house. Richard knocked at the door which was opened by a maid. He explained that he had a message for the owner of the house, and was shown into a room where two elderly ladies were entertaining friends.

Clarke introduced himself and told them he had come from Hannington in Northamptonshire. The two old ladies became excited and said that their family had originally come from that village, and that their name was Pell. Soon afterwards their guests left and Pell's ghost materialised. The women shrieked, but Clarke calmed them and told them as gently as he could, the reason for his visit and Pell's request. Their reaction was sceptical especially when the buried treasure was mentioned. The spirit grew angry and destroyed a heavy round table in the room. At this the ladies became quiet and sensibly said that they believed what Clarke had told them.

Pell then led them down to the cellar, where he instructed Clarke to dig down six feet with an iron spade. Clarke dug until he was some feet down, then protested that he was tired and refused to dig deeper. The ghost told him to carry on, as he must be nearly there. Clarke's spade hit something hard: it was a metal box which, to Richard's amazement, when opened contained hundreds of gold and silver coins, turned black with age. The papers fell to dust when exposed to the air, but the parchment documents were still intact, and the dates and names, which were still legible, verified the truth of Pells' story. Then the spirit instructed Clarke how to dispose of the money. The main beneficiaries were the two old ladies who lived in the house, for as Pell explained they were his direct descendants.

After all his instructions were carried out Pell was able to rest in peace and Clarke and his family were no longer haunted by the restless ghost.

NORTHUMBERLAND

The Haunting of Willington Mill

Quaker Joseph Proctor and his family moved into the mill house of Willington Mill on Tyneside in 1835. It had recently been occupied for twenty-five years without incident by relatives of theirs, but later they heard that locally the place had a sinister reputation.

The family had scarcely settled in before the alarming disturbances which were to mark the whole of their occupation began. The nursemaid was putting the children to bed in their second floor room when she heard heavy footsteps tramping overhead, and the sound of furniture being moved. As far as she knew the third floor was empty. The sounds continued night after night, and the room was searched but no intruder found.

There was no let-up in the noise of heavy footsteps, thumps and whistling, and one morning when Mr Proctor was conducting family prayers the footsteps were heard coming downstairs, along the hall, and up to the front door, where the lock was apparently turned and the bolts drawn. Mr Proctor hurried out into the hall and found the front door open and the sound of footsteps continuing down the path. But there was no one to be seen, although that was to change.

Firstly, the maid, Mary Young, was washing up in the kitchen when she heard footsteps coming down the passage. She looked up and saw a woman in a silk dress go upstairs.

Then Mrs Proctor's sister came on a visit, and one night while they were sleeping together in one of the family's four-posters the whole bed levitated! A search was made underneath, but no one was there. Another night the bed was violently shaken and the bed curtains pulled up and down. They removed the curtains, but the next night when Mrs Proctor and her sister were lying awake they were terrified to see the misty, bluish figure of a woman emerge from the wall and lean over them, before disappearing back through the wall.

On another occasion Mrs Proctor was wakened when something cold was pressed hard against her eyes, which she found very frightening ...

One night the mill foreman and his family were returning home past the Proctors' house and saw a luminous figure appear to go through the wall of the second floor and then stand looking out of the window.

A psychic investigator, Edward Drury, and a friend were allowed to spend the night at the Proctors' in the summer of 1840. At about ten minutes to one Drury saw a closet door open and a woman in greyish clothing emerge, one hand pressed to her chest as if in pain. She came towards Drury, then turned, her arm pointing at his friend who was sleeping in a chair. Drury remembered rushing at the figure, and passing straight through before he fainted. He took some time to recover from the shock.

The children also encountered a ghostly figure and one said, 'There's a lady sitting on the bed in mama's room. She has eye-holes but no eyes, and she looked hard at me.'

As well as the grey lady, a voice was heard saying 'Chuck', and disconnected sentences like 'Come and get it' and 'Never mind'. The children saw a monkey, and several times a curious catlike white creature with a long pointed snout was seen disappearing through walls and doors, and once apparently into the engine-house fire.

Life became intolerable for the Proctors, and in 1847 after twelve years of poltergeist activity they moved out of the mill house at Willington, the mysterious entity giving them a farewell burst of violent noisy activity the night before.

Mr Proctor kept a diary in which he recorded their experiences, and this was published in 1892 in the Journal of the Society for Psychical Research. The mill was later turned into separate dwellings but although there were some strange happenings from time to time, nothing on the scale of the Proctors' ordeal recurred.

NOTTINGHAMSHIRE

Nottingham Castle

N ottingham Castle has had a long and chequered career. Sitting high up on an outcrop of sandstone, it occupies a natural defensive position but only the restored gatehouse and some foundations now remain of the Norman castle built around 1068. During the 'Anarchy of King Stephen' it was destroyed and rebuilt twice. In 1313 a band of the townspeople attacked the King's yeomanry in the castle and killed the Mayor. In the affray one of the rebels was captured and imprisoned in the castle until he was freed by a comrade who secretly gained entrance – echoes of Robin Hood? In 1335 there was another revolt, the castle gates were breached and the castle itself was besieged for eight days. King Charles I raised the Stuart standard at the castle at the beginning of the English Civil War, but it ominously blew away that night in a storm. After the defeat of the Royalists the castle, like so many others, was 'slighted' on the orders of Cromwell and a fine baroque mansion took its place, built between 1674 and 1679 by the Duke of Newcastle. This house was completely gutted by fire in the Reform Bill riots of 1831 and remained a ruin until 1875. It was rescued by the Nottingham Corporation, and was restored and refurbished as the city's art gallery and museum. Despite its disappointing un-castle-like appearance, especially for those visitors seeking the romance of Robin Hood, the building has had both drama and mystery aplenty.

The castle is thoroughly haunted and beneath its rocky foundations are tunnels and secret passages. Underneath it, carved into the sandstone outcrop on which it stands, is the famous tunnel known as Mortimer's Hole. The passageway is eerie enough, made all the more so by the reputed presence of the ghost of Sir Roger Mortimer himself. Mortimer, the Earl of March and lover of Queen Isabella, was probably her accomplice in the murder of Edward II. On the night of 19th October 1330 the Queen and her lover were staying at Nottingham Castle. Seeking to bring his father's killer to justice and expose his feckless mother, the young King Edward III entered the network of secret tunnels that led ultimately into the castle itself. With a band of loyal supporters, the King burst into his mother's bedroom and surprised the lovers. Edward himself is said to have seized Mortimer. The now doomed regicide was led away, so legend has it, to Isabella's mournful cries of 'Fair son, have pity on the gentle Mortimer'. Sir Roger was imprisoned in the castle, then taken to London and executed as a traitor at Tyburn. He was hanged, drawn and quartered on 29th November 1330 and his wretched remains skewered on spikes and left to rot on Traitors' Gate. The tunnel that led to Sir Roger's downfall became known by his name. The castle's tunnels, as well as the extensive system of passages under the city, are open to the public and well worth a visit.

There are other ghosts connected with the castle. In 1212 King John held around 28 sons of Welsh noble families hostage there. The boys, some as young as twelve, lived at the castle for a considerable time, and were allowed free rein within the walls, then one day, the precise date is unknown, King John ordered that all the hostages should be executed. A chronicler states that the boys' pitiful cries rang around the castle as one after the other they were taken up on the ramparts and hanged in a row. Their ghostly pleas for mercy are still said to be heard within the castle precincts. In a newspaper article on the castle that appeared in the 1920s an elderly resident of Nottingham told of his boyhood home in Castle Gate that was plagued by ghosts. It was believed by his family that they were haunted by ghosts from the castle itself. How or why the ghosts 'went over the wall' was never explained and the haunting stopped as quickly as it started. There are also old accounts of the ghostly sounds of billiard balls clicking late at night at Newdigate House in Castle Gate. Phantom voices and footsteps heard in the entrance hall further suggest that the house is haunted.

❖

The Trip to Jerusalem

Reputed to be the oldest pub in England, the Trip to Jerusalem in Nottingham is thought to have been built in 1189. It was a favourite watering hole for the Crusaders on their way to the Holy Land and Richard the Lionheart is said to have stayed here on one of his brief stops in England. The word 'Trip' or 'Trypp' comes, we are told, from an old word for halt or stop. Much of the fabric of the building is carved out from the rock on which the castle above stands and the walls and ceilings are bedecked with all manner of curios and antiques, some dating back to the Civil War. The lighting casts weird shadows about, and the Trip has an atmosphere to which written description cannot do justice - it must be experienced. Patrick Dare and his wife Marilyn became managers of the pub in February 1994. Marilyn knows much of the pub's strange history and has had weird experiences there of her own.

In the Rock Lounge was a model galleon which had hung from the ceiling for the past 150 years. It was covered in dust and cobwebs but no one would ever volunteer to clean it because it was said to be cursed. And according to Marilyn, 'The last three people who cleaned it are said to have died mysterious and unexpected deaths within twelve months of doing so.'

This model was one of several hanging from the ceiling, all thought to be parting gifts from sailors who had made them to pass the time at sea, like the scrimshaw of the whalers. Nottingham was once a busy inland port, the river Trent being navigable for quite large vessels all the way to the Humber and the North Sea. Nothing was known of the sinister galleon's maker or its history, and it continued to hang from the ceiling of the Rock Lounge, completely shrouded in the thick dust of ages as in view of its reputation no one would risk touching it.

But in 1996 the pub's owners were faced with a dilemma. The ancient

Medium Mallory Stendall with the 'cursed' galleon

hostelry was due for a £4 million refit and obviously someone had to take down the 150 year old model galleon, curse or no curse, so that the work could go ahead. The brewery was unwilling to put the builders at risk so it was decided that a medium should be consulted, Mallory Stendall, who proved equal to the daunting task. Mrs Stendall performed a ceremony of exorcism and then took down the galleon without disaster. With admirable calm she said, 'I'm not in the least bit nervous. I believe in my faith in God.' And the galleon was safely replaced once the work was completed.

The Rock Lounge in particular seems to have always been a focal point for odd happenings. Things such as keys have disappeared only to turn up later in odd places. Glasses and bottles have been known to fly off the shelves and smash, when no one is near by. Staff have heard the sound of breaking glass coming from the bar, but when they've gone with a dustpan and brush to clear it up, they simply can't find any. Sometimes a waft of perfume has filled the air, described as old-fashioned scent, like lavender or rose water.

Marilyn and Patrick were informed that the pub was haunted when they arrived. 'We were told that a group of tourists had asked to see the cellars and they saw two foot-soldiers walk through a wall. This was seen by the whole party, a group of five people. A medium visited the pub and she told us that a clock hanging in the bar was possessed by two evil spirits. A previous landlady had two Dobermanns that hated that clock. They would stand and bark at it for no reason. Our Dobermann, Moritz, named after Baron von Richthofen's deerhound, howled whenever we put him in the office. This is an entrance to Mortimer's Hole and they say animals are very sensitive to atmosphere. Previous landlords have both seen and heard two ghosts, a man and a woman. We hear people calling when there's no one there. The woman, wearing what appears to be crinoline skirts, is seen walking down the stairs into the cellars.'

Carved out from the soft rock, the cellars of the Trip to Jerusalem are like interconnecting caves. They have been in use at least since the Norman Conquest and probably longer. A narrow shaft pierces the rock above all the way up to the castle. It is believed this was a 'shouting hole' to allow those in the castle to call for more ale from the cellars below. In one chamber in the cellars a horseshoe-shaped bench has been cut into the rock around the walls; this was a cockfighting pit. According to Marilyn, 'Sometimes you can smell tallow burning down there. They used this for candles. The smell can linger for 20 minutes and then it's suddenly gone.'

On the far side of the cellars a rusting iron gate hangs limply from its hinges before a doorway cut into the rock wall. This is said to be the condemned cell of the castle prison. A curious green mould grows on the walls and ceiling. A rock bench has been carved out on one wall, offering cold comfort to the unfortunate inmates. The condemned cell isn't used to store beer as the ceiling is too low; for the most part it is kept empty. There is something more to the cell's oppressive atmosphere than its natural chill – there is a palpable cloud of doom here. Marilyn concurs with this, 'As you walk in the cell, you know it's not right, you know it is evil. Men condemned to death were shackled to the walls in there. Some left to die of starvation or dehydration. Two of the pub's regulars, full of Dutch courage, once decided they would spend the night in the condemned cell. They lasted 20 minutes, and were violently sick afterwards. My husband had some eerie experiences down there, not long after we'd moved in. The mallets for tapping the barrels kept disappearing. These are big rubber ones that are always kept in the same place. Sometimes you go down there and you can't find one anywhere, only to look again to see the three mallets lined up on three consecutive barrels, where you've just looked. One day he needed to get something from the other side of the cellar. He didn't bother to turn the light on and as he crossed he room something icy touched him lightly on the back of his neck. Needless to say the lights are always on now if anyone is working in there.

'Sometime later I was working at the sink, near the condemned cell, washing some buckets out, when I saw something walk past me. There was no one else there and it couldn't have been a shadow, it was like a grey mass. I had this feeling like an icy bar being passed through my body. I just stood there totally still. Then I looked at my feet because I felt this iciness come down and go out through my toes and I shuddered from head to foot. I don't know whether it was a condemned prisoner that hasn't passed over properly, or a soul in torment but it was a totally evil feeling, horrible. I wouldn't go down there again for about three weeks. It really frightened me.'

❖

For Sale – Secondhand Car . . .

From a librarian in Edwinstowe comes this story of a haunted car. A young local couple were looking to buy themselves a family car. The husband worked at the nearby pit and his wife had a part-time job in the village. They wanted something affordable and practical, 'a good clean motor'. With these requirements in mind, they toured the local car dealers' forecourts. On a Saturday morning in November they found a vehicle to meet all their needs, a hatchback, in excellent condition, at a very good price. The husband was a little suspicious, the paint was too new, he suspected a re-spray, the mileage was very low for a car of this registration. He spoke to the dealer who informed him that it was entirely genuine, the car had only just arrived and was priced for a quick sale. After a test drive the couple decided to buy it. Terms were agreed and the dealer promised to forward the log book as soon as he received it in the post.

All went well and the car proved an excellent 'runner'. The husband's change of shifts meant that he had the car mostly but, when convenient, his wife would drop him off at the pit and have the car to herself. On a dank morning, before seven, the tired miner drove home. He'd done some overtime and was looking forward to a hot bath and a long sleep. Up ahead a milk float stopped on his side of the road. Checking in the rearview mirror before pulling out, he saw something large lurch from one side of the car's back seat to the other. Startled, he turned his head to see, illuminated by the yellow neon glow of the street lights, a horribly disfigured corpse, whose dead eyes looked straight at him. He slammed on the brakes, narrowly missing the milk float. Transfixed, he stared at the hideously injured body. In terror he leapt from the car and ran up the road to the milk float. It was some minutes before he could make the startled milkman understand there was a body on the back seat of his car. Cautiously they walked back to the abandoned vehicle, together they gingerly peered through the rear window, there was nothing there. They searched the immediate area – nothing. Sympathetically, the milkman suggested that perhaps the miner had been working too hard and had experienced some sort of hallucination. Calmer now, the miner agreed and continued his on his way home, deciding to say nothing to his wife as she might worry.

On the day shift once more, it was his wife's turn to have the car. After a busy morning at work and with the week's shopping to do, she called in at a petrol station to fill up. Whilst paying at the counter her attention was suddenly drawn to her car. 'There's someone stealing my car,' she cried and dashed across the forecourt. Grabbing open the door, she froze in horror as a body, terribly mutilated, fell out onto the tarmac. Screaming, she ran back into the garage shop. The equally terrified assistant calmed her down and rang for the police. Both were too disturbed to approach the car themselves and waited for the arrival of the police. To their relief, they were quick to respond. However, the officers found no trace of a body, no blood, no signs of violence, nothing. The policemen, understandably, insisted on a breath test. This proved negative, and after the careful reassurance of the officers, the lady went home. On collecting her husband from work, she was surprised by his grave and silent attention to her story.

'I didn't want to tell you this,' he said, 'but I saw the same thing but thought I'd imagined it.' Later that same evening a policeman visited the couple. He informed them that the car had been run through the police computer. It had been in a fatal accident. It hadn't been 'written off', as only the rear of the car was damaged in a freak accident with a lorry that left a passenger dead. The next morning an envelope arrived in the post.

It was the log book, showing the car had had six previous owners in two years. Immediately they decided to get rid of it. That same morning the husband returned to the car dealer and he was offered two hundred pounds less for the car than he paid for it. He accepted the offer without hesitation, and the dealer asked no questions. Perhaps the car is waiting now on some forecourt – 'For Sale – Excellent Condition – Haunted'. A modern myth or a cautionary tale? Either way, *caveat emptor*, let the buyer beware.

OXFORDSHIRE

The Ghost With Red Hair

There are sad stories behind many hauntings, and this is no exception. But it is also the story of a man who fell romantically in love with a beautiful ghost.

In the Dorchester Abbey Church is a plain slab with this inscription:

*Reader! If thou hast a heart famed for Tenderness
And Pity, Contemplate this Spot in which are deposited
The remains of a Young Lady whose artless beauty,
Innocence of mind, and gentle manners once obtained
Her the love and esteem of all who knew her. But when
Nerves were too delicately spun to bear the rude shakes
And jostlings which we meet with in this transitory world,
Nature gave way; she sunk and died, a martyr to excessive
Sensibility.*

MRS SARAH FLETCHER

Wife of Captain Fletcher, departed this life
at the village of Clifton on the 7th June
1799 in the 29th year of her age.
May her soul meet that peace in Heaven which this earth
denied her.

But Sarah Fletcher did not rest in peace. Her spirit haunted her former home, 'Courtiers'; in the village of Clifton Hampden, for many years.

Sarah was married to a naval officer, a man with a roving eye who apparently had become so involved with a rich heiress that he was on the point of a bigamous marriage when Sarah heard about it, and was just in

Courtiers in Clifton Hampden, the scene of Sarah Fletcher's unhappy death in 1799

time to stop proceedings. It is easy to imagine the dramatic confrontation, and recriminations, which caused the infamous Captain Fletcher to make a hasty retreat in the direction of his ship, from where he set sail for the West Indies, leaving the two ladies to cope as best they could.

Sarah returned home in such a desperately unhappy state of mind that she took her own life by tying her handkerchief to a piece of cord and hanging herself from the curtain rail of her bed.

Maude Ffoulkes, who compiled *True Ghost Stories* with the Marchioness Townshend, visited the Abbey Church one summer day in

1913 and was intrigued by Sarah's story. She visited Courtiers, now an institution, but her enquiries about a ghost drew a blank. However, as she glanced down a passageway she saw a woman wearing a black cloak looking back at her. She had auburn hair tied with a ribbon, and her white face and anguished eyes made Maude feel that she was actually seeing the ghost of Sarah Fletcher.

Not much later her desire to know more was satisfied when she met a clergyman, Edward Crake, who had once lived in Courtiers and who shared her deep interest in Sarah Fletcher. He told Maude that his father was a schoolmaster, and when he was ten years old, his father had rented Courtiers at an amazingly low rent, needing somewhere larger for his school and family. They soon discovered that previous tenants had never stayed there long, the property had an eerie reputation, but Mr Crake made it clear that he wanted no silly gossip about ghosts, which could be to the detriment of the school.

For this reason Edward knew nothing about Sarah Fletcher until the night he actually saw her ghost, and fell in love with her.

It was a moonlit night, Edward was 17 and he was lying in bed awake when he heard approaching footsteps, his bedroom door opened and he felt that someone unseen had entered, hesitated and gone out again. He heard the church clock strike three, and then as nothing else transpired he fell asleep.

The next night everything happened in just the same way, and he decided that the following night he would be ready to find out who or what the unseen intruder might be. Sure enough, just as before he heard the footsteps, and this time he felt sure it was the sound of someone in high heeled shoes. Once again the footsteps entered his room, approached his bed and then retreated. Edward jumped out of bed and ran out into the corridor which was brightly lit by moonlight, and there, for the first time he saw Sarah, standing by a window.

'She seemed tremendously alive,' he said. 'There was nothing "dead" about her. Her eyes were full of tears, she had come from the edge of the world, and from soundless space, to seek my love and pity.'

Maude asked what she looked like, anxious to confirm that when she visited Courtiers she, too, had seen the ghost of Sarah Fletcher.

'She wore a black silk cloak, fashionable at that period for protecting ladies' dresses from the dust of the roads ... she was hatless, and her hair was twined about with a purple-red ribbon ... I wanted to help her, to befriend her – then all at once a patch of moonlight alone marked the place where she had stood.'

Enquiries showed that other people in the house were aware of the ghostly footsteps and an assistant master told Edward that once when he was going upstairs, the footsteps approached him and he felt a cold wind pass by. On another occasion he heard the footsteps approach his bed and saw a cloudlike mass which really frightened him.

Edward satisfied his curiosity about the lovely phantom by talking to a very old gentleman in the village who still remembered her 'artless beauty'. He also found a report of the inquest on 15th June 1799 which had reached a verdict of Lunacy which made it possible for her to be buried in consecrated ground in the church. Edward and his friend, the assistant master, arranged to sit up one night and keep a vigil on the anniversary of her death.

At the usual time of quarter to three they heard footsteps descending the stairs, and when his friend's courage failed him, Edward went on alone, hoping no doubt that once again he might see the beautiful Sarah. And it happened. As he told Maude, 'Between the dawn on the one hand and the moon on the other, I saw her again. This time she smiled at me, and her face had lost something of its tragic intensity ... She turned the handle of the door, opened it and I ran towards her ... she was so real that I could not believe I was in the presence of someone dead in the body for many years. "Speak to me," I begged, "please, please speak to me." But the door closed in my face, and when I pushed it open the room was empty except for a few boys sleeping quietly, unconscious of the phantom which had passed by.'

There were more occasional sightings of Sarah, and at other times Edward, still obsessed with his romantic dreams of the beautiful auburn haired ghost, sensed her nearness. Then, after about a year, the footsteps ceased, and there was a quieter, more peaceful atmosphere in the house.

Ten years later when Edward's brother had become the Headmaster of the school at Courtiers, and he himself was now a clergyman, he received a letter from his brother asking him to come, as ghostly activity at the house had begun again in a more troublesome form. Occupants had been frightened by a presence at their bedside, and there was a lot of knocking and other noises.

Edward once again was captivated by a sighting of Sarah, and felt that although there now seemed to be a malevolent power in the haunting, she was not the cause. But he could not ignore the violent disturbances and attempted an exorcism which seemed to have a calming effect.

But this was shortlived, and the occupants often found themselves listening to what seemed to be noisy furniture being moved about overhead. Things came to a head when there was an outbreak of fever in the village, including the school, and in desperation Edward's brother decided to leave Courtiers and move his school to another town.

Afterwards there were many tenants and considerable alterations to Courtiers over the years and it eventually became a private residence again. Edward Crake, who died in 1915, gave a report on the haunting of his old home to the Society for Psychical Research, but not his secret dreams about Sarah Fletcher which he had confided to Maude Ffoulkes. Is the sound of those little high heeled shoes still heard in the house where beautiful Sarah knew so much unhappiness? Does anyone now see the beautiful ghost with ribbons in her auburn hair? Who knows?

RUTLAND

The Ghosts of Stocken Hall

S tocken Hall on the outskirts of Stretton is home to no less than three ghosts. One is a woman dressed in black who lowers her head to hide her face as she flits down a corridor. In the early part of the 19th century she was seen quite frequently, by visitors as well as by the occupants of the Hall, but if spoken to she immediately vanished. She is believed to be the ghost of a girl who was strangled in the attic.

The ghost of a small white dog was also often seen and on one occasion a woman and her daughter were going up a narrow staircase when the dog passed them so closely that both said afterwards that they felt it brush past their legs, but they knew it was not a real animal as it appeared to be semi-transparent.

The third apparition is of a more terrifying kind and was seen several times. One report is of a December day when three people from the Hall were crossing the park. Their dog showed signs of being frightened by something, and they then noticed the figure of a man hanging from the bough of an oak tree. He was wearing a brown smock with something white covering his face, and as they drew nearer he disappeared. It is known that a man was murdered there in the early 19th century after he had been accused of sheep stealing.

Stocken Hall is now an open prison.

Mysteries at Stoke Dry

T he ancient church of St Andrew at Stoke Dry is an atmospheric and mysterious place. Inside, a narrow stairway leads to a small room above the church porch which was a priest's room or parvis. Local legend has it that the Gunpowder plot was hatched in this room, but there is another old story that a rector of St Andrews church once imprisoned a woman alleged to be a witch in the parvis where she died of starvation. Some accounts say that her spirit haunts the place where she suffered such a cruel death, but if you visit the church you will find a notice at the foot of the stairs leading to the room which asserts that there is no truth in this chilling rumour.

SHROPSHIRE

The Haunting of Dorothy Blount

I t has been said that death is a great leveller, but Squire Blount of Kinlet Hall refused to admit it. Class distinction was important to him in death as well as in life.

Sir George was squire of Kinlet and of Bewdley, and a very rich man by all accounts. When his curly haired young son lost his life (through choking on an apple core, alas) the squire could do no more for him than to provide a silver coffin, and the tragedy left his daughter, Dorothy, as heir to Kinlet Hall with a fairly substantial fortune. Her future status then became of paramount importance to her father and he was incensed when she broke the news that she intended (in his eyes) to 'marry beneath her'. Yet she had fallen in love – not with a dashing young Romeo, as one might suppose, but with a widower named John Parslowe, a country gentleman, but untitled.

Sir George would have none of it! The worst side of his nature came into play (apparently he could be quite courteous and well controlled when it suited him) and he threatened not only to disinherit his daughter, but to return to haunt her and any children of the marriage if she persisted in her obstinacy. When the marriage did take place he made a new will, naming the issue of his sister Agnes as his heirs, and he kept up his bitter recriminations against his daughter until the end of his life.

At his death in 1581 he was given a magnificent tomb in the north transept of Kinlet church with an effigy of himself kneeling alongside his wife, with their two children placed between them. A touching picture of family life! But misleading, and the aftermath makes for high drama.

A group of local women were innocently swilling their washing in a pool near the Hall when, they claimed, they were confronted by the astonishing spectacle of the squire rising out of the depths on horseback and charging straight towards them. They scattered, of course, and he disappeared. But the next appearance was still more bizarre. He was reported to have surfaced, crouched on the edge of the driving seat of his coach, furiously speeding the four horses over the grounds and through the rooms of Kinlet Hall. He then swept into the dining room and up over the dinner table where Dorothy and guests were peacefully partaking of their evening meal!

Unfortunately this was not a one off, and in time the pool was abandoned by the washerwomen and the Hall itself demolished and rebuilt. All to no avail. Still the sightings continued. Eventually the priests were called in to exorcise his restless spirit.

But what a battle they had. Each brought a lighted candle and placed it on a long oak table. Then followed the recital of a long lesson, and prayers continued until all candles but one had burnt out. Alongside this they placed a flat bottle especially designed for their purpose of driving the restless spirit inside. As the last candle flame died out they concluded the proceedings, assured in their hearts that the spirit of the unforgiving father had been captured and securely stoppered in the bottle. This was then conveyed to the Blount tomb in the church, sternly warning all and sundry that it must never be removed or tampered with to ensure the peace of Kinlet Hall and the parishioners!

It seems that the bottle stayed in place for many years, but that even after it finally disappeared (and was said to contain nothing but photographic fluid) the cantankerous squire appeared no more.

SOMERSET

The Grey Lady of
Sydenham Manor

S ydenham Manor is perhaps Bridgwater's best kept secret. Tucked away within the industrial complex of the Cellophane plant, the five hundred year old manor house has remained hidden for several decades. Sadly, access to this Tudor yeoman's estate is restricted and the Bridgwater public rarely, if ever, get to see this grade II listed building. But I was one of the lucky ones and was privileged to use it on a regular basis over a period of some thirty years.

Its history can be traced back to the Domesday Book. It came under attack during the English Civil War and it is reputed that the Duke of Monmouth stopped here to take a last meal and share prayers with his priest before embarking on his fateful and final campaign to capture the throne of England. The room he used is still known today as the Monmouth Room. Our ghost story has little to do with Monmouth but plenty to do with the room.

In its original form, the manor house was a single storey rectangular building, unlike its present day three storey L-shaped successor. It had been extended upwards and outwards over the generations. On the first floor there are five bedrooms and a lounge, one bedroom being Monmouth's room.

Over the years various visitors to the Manor, from all corners of the world, have slept within its walls. And every now and again a visitor will report a ghostly experience, but only ever those who stay in the Monmouth Room. The commonest manifestation is the appearance of the Grey Lady. Dressed in a long flowing robe, she drifts out of one corner of

Sydenham Manor, with its intriguingly haunted Monmouth Room

the room to exit by another, and in neither case does a door conveniently exist and hence she is obliged to pass through the walls. However, this phenomenon can be explained by the fact that, in its earlier days, the building had doors in the very places where the lady's wanderings suggest the doors should be.

Although on the first floor it is only the Monmouth Room that is affected by these visitations, but strange events also take place in the housekeeper's flat on the upper floor. These take the form of poltergeist behaviour with lights and taps going on and off, pictures moving and similar experiences. But Christine, the housekeeper, simply shouts to her guest 'Stop it. Go away,' and all returns to normal.

The Grey Lady does, however, appear to appreciate technology. Christine had bought a video to go with her television, but on the evening concerned preferred to sit down and read a book. The Grey Lady had other ideas – both television and video switched themselves on. The remote controls were on the floor, well away from human interference. The hairs stood up on Christine's neck!

Christine was given a little toy bird which would tweet when handled. It graced the dresser in Christine's bedroom until early on Saturday morning when it woke Christine with a non-stop string of twittering. It was then banished to the kitchen and now performs unprompted several times a week.

Further evidence of an acceptance of technology comes from the experience with the tea towels. These used to be hung on two lines in the kitchen of Christine's flat. The ghost's favourite game was to unhook the lines and scatter the towels on the floor. This practice continued until Christine acquired a tumble drier. But there was a limit to this acceptance of technology.

In the early 1990s, the Long Room in the Manor was set up with a number of PCs for a training course. The delegates were arriving at about 8.30 am when suddenly water started pouring in through the ceiling. There had been a guest in the bedroom immediately above the Long Room and perhaps therein lay the cause of the problem. But on examination it was realised that the bathroom linked to the bedroom was in the wrong position to be the cause of the leak.

The plumbers arrived and took up the floorboards immediately over the area where the water had poured through. The whole area was absolutely dry and on re-examining the ceiling, there were no water marks at all. The mess was cleaned up, the floor dried and all returned to normal – until a few weeks later. Another computer course had been set up, water once again poured through the same place in the ceiling and again, on investigation, nothing was found.

The Grey Lady, apart from her mixed views on modern technology, appears to be a friendly ghost – with one rare exception. A visitor from a training organisation was staying in the Monmouth Room and woke in the morning to find three shallow razor-like cuts in close parallel formation down one cheek, and yet this was a gentleman who only used an electric razor and there was no evidence of a conventional razor in the room. Nor was he aware of having his face cut during his night's rest other than by seeing the cuts in the morning.

The bedding was completely changed, and the mattress turned over, in case there had been a foreign body with a sharp edge somewhere in the furniture or laundry. Despite these safeguards, the following night his other cheek was cut in similar fashion.

An electrician who was often obliged to visit the Monmouth Room to replace one of the many light bulbs was unable to open its door. It was as if he were a persona non grata and consequently the housekeeper would open the door for him. He would then place his toolbox in the open doorway and overcome the problem that way.

A German visitor in the same room felt the need, one hot summer's night, to close the window which he claimed was rattling in the wind. But these were heavy duty windows which I have failed to make rattle no matter how hard I have tried. On reaching the windows he was raised off the floor by a blast of air which shot him across the room, hitting the wall on the far side, just next to the door, in what appears to be a levitation experience.

Gathering himself together, he rapidly escaped through the door and headed for the lounge where he spent the rest of the night. In the morning Christine was obliged to collect the visitor's personal belongings. There was no way he would re-enter the room on that visit.

By strange coincidence, I was studying the history of Sydenham Manor and found a reference to a George Sydenham who in the 14th century had been levitated from the very same building to the top of a tree in the grounds of the manor house.

On one occasion we had an open day at the Manor when I was on duty downstairs and a colleague, Helen, was on duty in the Monmouth Room. Needless to say many visitors enquired as to the ghost and Helen and myself told the occasional tale.

It was mid afternoon when an ashen faced Helen ran down the stairs, visibly distressed, declaring that the wardrobe in the Monmouth Room had attacked two of our visitors. The way Helen described the event was that the wardrobe had violently thrown open its doors, knocking two gentlemen guests in their backs and sent them hurtling to a soft landing on the bed in the middle of the room. When Helen described to me the sequence of events, I confess I gave little credence to her version of affairs but subsequent happenings have completely changed my beliefs.

A year or so after that episode, a teacher from a nearby primary school contacted me to arrange for a group of his pupils to visit the Manor. They were eight years old and there were about a hundred of them. It was too many to take in one go, so we agreed to take them in six groups and to ferry them to and fro by minibus.

The day of the visit arrived and the first group of children were safely delivered. I tried to explain how the house was five hundred years old, but it meant little to these youngsters who were far more interested in meeting the ghost. Explaining to them that she was unlikely to appear with so many visitors, I took them up the Monmouth Room and there they sat on the bed or on the floor and listened intently while I retold stories about the lady ghost.

To warm them up, I explained how the Duke of Monmouth was executed in the Tower of London and how his portrait that hung on the wall, in that very room, was a copy of one painted after his execution, and required his head to be stitched back before he 'sat' for the artist! And it was an execution which went terribly wrong. After the first swing of the executioner's axe, the Duke was able to turn his head and glower at the axeman, the corner of the blade having caught the block while the face of the blade penetrated no more than an inch into the Duke's head. A second attempt to sever his head was likewise unsuccessful and the Duke was seen to twist his legs in agony. Even a third attempt failed to completely sever the head and the axeman was obliged to finish the job with a knife.

Having thus gained the full attention of my visitors, I related stories of the lady ghost and the various other ghostly experiences. As I talked of the Duke's portrait, I looked towards the portrait. When I talked of the window, I looked to the window. So I was not in a position to observe the wardrobe until I told its story and in turn it came under my attention.

As I turned to look at the wardrobe, I saw the wooden handles were slowly rocking, very deliberately and quite unnaturally. I sought some scientific explanation involving my weight plus the combined weight of sixteen eight year olds, and how we had applied pressure to the five hundred year old floor – surely it was somehow related to that.

When I received the second group of children, I kept a close watch on the wardrobe. As I talked of the Duke, and the window, and the corners of the room through which passed the Grey Lady, I never once took my eyes off the wardrobe. Not a twitch came from the handles. But the instant I mentioned its behaviour on our open day, the wardrobe began its performance. The handles slowly and deliberately rocked back and forth.

On receiving the third group, and still convinced this had to be a natural rather than supernatural phenomenon, I worked on the theory that it was all to do with the passing of time, from when the children entered the room to when I related the wardrobe's story. That had to be the determining factor in the wardrobe's movements and it was purely coincidental that it happened when I mentioned the wardrobe.

So with the third group, and likewise with the next three, I swapped the stories around to vary the time in the room before I related the wardrobe's tale. Each and every time I mentioned the wardrobe, it performed on cue. As soon as I mentioned the open day, it rocked its handles to and fro. I was now beginning to believe Helen's story. But further proof was yet to come of the credibility of her account.

The following year, with some reservations, I received another school party but this time with no unexpected visitations. So I put my concerns behind me and had forgotten the matter by the time a local Round Table group came to the Manor. The purpose of their visit was to hear a talk on the house, its characters and its history. The lecture over, the inevitable question surfaced. 'Can we see the haunted room?' And so I took the group up into the Monmouth Room and there related tales of previous encounters. With no warning whatsoever, the lights in the room went off and as rapidly back on at exactly the same moment that the wardrobe thrust open its doors attacking two of my guests. It was an exact repeat of Helen's experience which previously I treated with more than a drop of scepticism.

A round of spontaneous applause broke out in the room as my visitors showed their appreciation for what they saw as a perfectly executed end to a very entertaining evening. And I was left totally bemused and somewhat unnerved.

This incident for me was the turning point where I was converted from sceptic to someone with a far more open mind.

I have never heard an explanation as to who the lady ghost could be but so many visitors have shared the same experience that it leaves little doubt as to her presence. Christine, the housekeeper, seems destined to share her home with the Grey Lady for as long as she remains, and indeed to be tormented along with her assistants. Almost without exception, when alone in the house, they each have heard their names called. On going to the first floor, to find whoever was calling, they have all found the door to the Monmouth Room alone to be open and not another soul present in the house. That is, apart from the Grey Lady.

Things that Go Bump in the Night

O f all the tales I have gathered, the following is the one which enthralled me the most, perhaps because of the lingering question mark left at the end of the tale. Just what was it, the strange unexplained being which left a former Marine Commando experiencing the most terrifying encounter of his life! The story unfolds high on the Mendip Hills, at Charterhouse, well known to many a group of adventurous school children who have attended residential visits there.

Lying on a trackway which leads from the old Roman road across the Mendips to a valley called Velvet Bottom, Charterhouse was once a small mining community of some fifty households, also a church, a pub and a school. These are all long gone save the old church and school which survives as part of the Charterhouse centre now owned by Somerset County Council as an educational establishment for outdoor pursuits.

The former classrooms have now been converted to meeting rooms and chalets have been added for accommodation. The headmistress's premises have been converted, downstairs to offices and upstairs to two bedrooms, one being used as a sick bay should a young student require observation or isolation, and the other for a member of staff.

Terry, the warden, had found a number of coins over the years, confirming the presence of the Romans who mined in the area for lead and silver. The whole area around Charterhouse provides evidence of the multitude of mines, the landscape littered with bumps and dips where ore was extracted and the spoil dumped.

By the start of the 19th century, it was just lead that was mined and smelted. It was realised that much of the lead was lost in the smelting process, carried away in the fumes and smoke. To recapture some of this, a system of horizontal chimneys, many yards long, was constructed. As the smoke passed through, the lead was deposited in the ash. All that was required was for the young orphan boys imported from Bristol to climb through these chimneys scraping out the deposits, lining their lungs with toxic waste as they did so. Life expectancy was short indeed for these poor wretches. But perhaps their souls lived on.

Richard Gardner was a teacher at Haygrove School in Bridgwater when he was part of a school expedition to Charterhouse in February 1982. On an early trip from the centre, the fifteen year olds were split into groups, each having two teachers in charge. One teacher stayed with the group as they trekked from the centre, down Velvet Bottom and Black Rock to cross the road which runs down through Cheddar Gorge. Beyond there, their journey continued up the other side of the gorge to the cliff top path down into Cheddar via Jacobs Ladder.

Richard's role on this trip was to drive ahead in a van to the road crossing point and check that all five students in his group were present and correct. Alas the group of five girls arrived one short. Maria had disappeared on the way and the other four girls had failed to search for her. Richard waited until all four had passed and the teacher bringing up the rear had arrived. She was unaware of Maria's whereabouts and clearly Maria had not lagged behind but rather left the route somewhere. Richard agreed to return to the centre and see if Maria had returned alone.

Maria was not to be found so Richard drove as far as he could down towards Velvet Bottom and there by a scout hut, now in driving rain with the wind blowing hard, he stepped out of the van to call her name. Calling and then listening intently for a response, Richard heard the sounds of young children, those happy playground sounds of skipping games and singing.

This was an isolated area, the nearest village being some five miles away. The bleak open landscape offered little opportunity to conceal any such group. The joyful sounds lingered and so Richard called for the assistance of the young lad waiting in his van, unable to make the long walk due to a leg problem. Asked what he could hear, the boy described the same experience, children laughing and singing. No explanation has ever been found. Perhaps these were the voices of the young Bristol orphans from a previous time.

On their return to the centre, Maria was found to be there ahead of them – safe and well. Realising she was lost, she simply retraced her steps. The mystery of the children's voices remained just that – a mystery.

But an even deeper mystery was looming. Terry, the warden of the centre, who was not usually present on such occasions, happened to be there that same evening. With the mystery of the singing children unresolved, the conversation around the fire that evening turned to ghost stories. Tales were exchanged and Terry was asked to contribute.

Now Terry was described to me as an ex-Marine, not prone to flights of fancy. He was a well disciplined, tough individual, in the true mould of the British Marine. He also had those qualities of leadership which instilled discipline just by an infection of the voice, a man people believed and respected. The children all thought well of him and pressed him incessantly. It was a reluctant Terry who revealed his own experience.

The centre, as well as serving an educational purpose, is also used by the Mendip Cave Rescue Team and equipment is stored there associated with caving activity. It had been a year earlier when Terry was at the centre, alone, in order to clean up the heavily used equipment and recharge the batteries for the many lights which were used in the caves. He knew he had hours of work ahead of him and hence telephoned his wife to say he'd be staying over.

At about ten in the evening, he called it a day, made a bowl of soup, watched the TV news and headed for bed. Collecting a sleeping bag, he went to the sick bay and made use of a bunk there, soon falling asleep with his back to the door and facing the outside wall.

At about one in the morning, he awoke to the sound of an animal snuffling around in the leaves and grass outside. Assuming it to be an old badger, he was just dropping off again, when the noise interrupted his sleep once more. This time it was not from in front of him, beyond the outer wall, but much closer and more distinct. It was from behind him, downstairs and within the building, within the hall.

He was convinced he had locked all the doors. He knew he had. Years of operating in a disciplined environment made such chores a matter of course. But if the doors were secure, how could an animal have got inside? Could he have left a door not properly locked? He found it hard to believe anything could have got in. What should he do? 'Blow it,' he thought, 'leave it until the morning.' Whatever this animal was, if it found its way in, it would find its own way out.

But then he could hear the noise of the animal ascending the stairs, coming closer and closer, snuffling and scratching around as it did so, until it reached the landing and was outside his room, snuffling at the foot of the door.

Terry now became alarmed. This was not normal behaviour for a wild animal. To enter an inhabited building is unusual, but the Charterhouse centre was often left unattended. Perhaps this abnormally large-sounding badger had become accustomed to exploring within when no one else was there. Whatever the explanation, Terry was now becoming unnerved, sensing something ominous and threatening was about to occur.

Then the sound changed from scratching and snuffling to something quite different. Imagine one of those hard-wearing coconut hair doormats, bristles erect. Imagine the sound of such an item being squeezed under the half inch gap at the bottom of a door, its hard knotted bottom dragging over wooden floorboards whilst the bristles brushed and scraped across the bottom of the door, and then the sounds of being dragged through by pulling and tugging from side to side until finally the last inch broke free.

This was the sound of a large creature being squeezed under the half inch gap at the bottom of the door behind him and into his room. It was impossible but he knew from the sound that this is what had just happened. Panic seized him as he lay facing the wall, fearing what might happen next, with the noise coming ever closer to his bed.

Then the sound of the scratching and sniffing was immediately behind him, within inches of his body. During all his army years, he had never, ever experienced terror like this, because there was no known explanation as to what was happening. So he lay in terror when the whole bed began to lurch violently. He reached out to grab on to anything he could clutch to try and steady the bed.

Grabbing something in the dark, he knew not what, he wrestled against the thrusting and jerking of the bed for some thirty seconds until the violent motions ceased and the scratching and snuffling began again as the creature made its way back towards the door. Then the sound changed to that of the creature dragging its way back under the door, then the snuffling and scratching as it descended the stairs, through the hall, and out beyond the walls of the building, across the yard and off into the night, fading away into complete silence. What on earth could this have been – this entity unknown to science?

A glance at the luminous hands on his watch showed it was now two in the morning. A terrifying hour had passed since the start of his ordeal. As much as he desperately wanted to understand the experience and know just what sort of creature behaved like this, there was no way he would open the sick room door that night, not until daylight.

Sleep returned but not until some considerable time had passed, and then morning broke. Terry, waking, turned on his pillow to feel something hard and gritty beneath his head. Recollecting the events of the previous night, common sense screamed at him that it had to have been a dream. But there on his pillow, and all over his bed, were chunks of plaster torn from the wall. It had been the electric cabling running down the wall which he had clasped in those hours of darkness wrestling against the violent behaviour as his bed was thrown around. All the cable clips had been pulled from the wall. This had been no dream and can be added to the other episode as yet another unresolved Charterhouse mystery.

Terry's story told, the children must have wished they had never pressed him to reveal the details of his encounter. That night, they all slept in the chairs and settees around the room in which the stories were exchanged, no one daring to cross the yard to the accommodation block.

A year later, when another group arrived, Terry slipped a note to their teacher, who had been present on the previous occasion when he had told the story of his intruder. It read:

'My visitor returned last week!'

STAFFORDSHIRE

The Ghost in the Ladies Loo

Margaret Buckle, known affectionately to everyone on the estate as 'Mrs B', had worked at Alton Towers for over 12 years before she saw the ghost in 1978. For four or five weeks she had thought that someone was playing tricks on her as she worked in the toilet building. She would be cleaning the wash basins when she would hear the outside door bang, then one of the toilet cubicle doors would close. Each time, Mrs B would call out 'Good morning' but would receive no reply. She decided that one of her colleagues was playing a joke on her, and she was determined to catch them at it.

The next time it happened, as she shouted 'Good morning', she whirled round to confront her tormenter. However, as usual there was no one there. Margaret carried on with her cleaning but suddenly she felt extremely cold, even though it was a pleasant warm day. She turned again and there before her she saw a figure wearing a black cloak, a floppy, big-brimmed black hat, and pointed toe boots with small black buttons up the side. In her own words, Mrs B 'took one look then ran like mad, nearly knocking over my boss, Mr Noaks'.

When she had recovered enough to be able to talk, Margaret told him what she'd seen, and was told not to worry as the ghost wouldn't hurt her. When she saw the ghost again, six weeks later, she shouted at it, 'Keep away from me. I'm not responsible for turning Alton Towers into what it is today!' The events occurred shortly after the stately home had begun to be developed into a leisure theme park with white-knuckle rides, pirate ships and fast-food restaurants. Mrs B believes that the cloaked figure might be a ghost from the past who does not approve of the changes.

The Alton Towers the ghostly visitor would have known

Although Mrs B couldn't tell whether her ghostly visitor was male or female, she had a feeling that it was a lady. Other staff have since seen her in the gift shop and near the Swiss Cottage in the gardens, and the ghost is often blamed for moving objects around. Visitors to Alton Towers have seen her by the moat, and some have even felt an invisible hand trying to push them off the low wall that borders the moat.

One theory is that she is the ghost of a young woman of high birth who was planning to run away with a young man of whom her family did not approve. The planned elopement was discovered and her father seized the young couple as they were about to ride off on horseback. He locked the girl in a tower, but she tried to escape by climbing through the tiny window. Tragically, she fell and was drowned in the moat. Most of the staff believe that she is the lady who appears dressed in her 19th century riding clothes, just as she was on the night of her failed elopement.

Driven from His Home

The strange phenomena which were experienced by Mr Wood and his cousin in a cottage in Longnor hit the national press. They also succeeded in driving Mr Wood from his home. Mr Wood had returned to the cottage after a stay in hospital, during which his elderly mother had died. In the early hours of 15th January 1960 he woke with the feeling that his own hand was being held by another, which was icy and invisible. He told himself that he was being silly, and that his imagination was playing tricks on him. Eventually he went back to sleep.

Over the next few nights, his sleep was disturbed by peculiar metallic noises, which he described as being like the sound of the handle of an iron bucket. Then one night a tremendous crash woke him. Convinced that a ceiling had collapsed in another bedroom, Mr Wood went to investigate but could not find the cause. The next morning he checked again, but all the rooms looked perfectly normal. An alarmed Mr Wood decided to spend a few days with friends in Leek. They tried to convince him that the strange events were all in his imagination.

When he returned to his cottage in Longnor, things appeared to have quietened down until a few weeks later when he heard what sounded like objects bumping on the stairs. When he checked he found that a number of empty cartons had indeed been thrown down the stairs.

His worst fright occurred one night when he saw the latch of his bedroom door lift. A white-haired old lady wearing a black cape passed through the room and vanished through the wardrobe. Mr Wood was terrified and slept with the light on after this event.

He made enquiries of his friends and relations, and his cousin Mrs Brittlebank told him of her own experiences in the cottage while he was in hospital. She had been staying there to look after her 80 year old aunt, Mr Wood's mother, during the final weeks of her life. She recalled one night when she had seen strange flickering lights which seemed to appear in one corner of the room, then dart about the room, finally coming to hover over the sleeping Mrs Wood. On another occasion, she had seen the bedroom door latch lift, and two figures enter the room then disappear. Both these phenomena had occurred shortly before Mrs Wood's death.

He also discovered that the previous owner of the cottage had experienced ghostly happenings, including one evening when a rug his wife was pegging was torn violently from her lap and hurled into the corner of the room. Their pet cat had fled in terror seconds before the event took place.

Mr Wood called in the services of a medium, who told him that there was a supernatural presence in the building, which had some connection with an old man and a dog. She also thought that there could be a body buried under the cottage.

Events began to get more frequent and more disturbing. Lights were switched on and off, heavy footsteps were heard, and the sound of a growling dog coming from the fireplace. Pots and pans seemed to be thrown about, there were sudden drops in temperature, and curtains were ripped down. Mrs. Brittlebank even had a cardigan torn from her shoulders.

The most terrifying event of all took place when Mr Wood was attempting to relay a flagstone in the floor. He had prised the flag up, and had begun to shovel soil from beneath it, when Mrs Brittlebank saw a horrific shape emerge from the ground, then leap away and disappear. It seemed to be a large dog.

Although the cottage was exorcised on more than one occasion, things were going from bad to worse. Mr Wood decided that he could live in his home no longer, and both he and his cousin moved out of the village to live in Leek.

SUFFOLK

The Strange Story of Corder's Skull

W hen author and ghost hunter R. Thurston Hopkins was young he lived in Gyves House, within the walls of the old prison at Bury St Edmunds. His father was an official in the Prison Service, and Hopkins recalled that at his home there was a framed letter, the last confession of William Corder, hanged on 11th August 1828 for the murder of Maria Marten.

Hopkins' father had a close friend, Dr Kilner, a Bury doctor with a rather macabre interest in the Red Barn Murder. In fact the former surgeon at Bury Jail, who bound a book about the murder in Corder's skin and also pickled Corder's scalp, bequeathed these grisly relics to Dr Kilner in his will.

But Dr Kilner also had a fancy to own Corder's skull which had been at the West Suffolk General Hospital for some fifty years, as part of the skeleton which was used for anatomy lessons. But how to acquire it? Dr Kilner, a well respected medical practitioner, decided there was nothing for it but a little midnight sleight of hand!

Hopkins' father, who later became involved, thoroughly enjoyed regaling family and guests at Christmastime with the macabre story of what happened next, every word of which he swore was absolutely true.

When Dr Kilner arrived at the hospital museum in the middle of the night to perform his skulduggery, he lit three candles. It was odd that one candle immediately went out, and as he relit it, the flames of the other two also vanished. As he removed the skull from Corder's skeleton, the candles kept up the same irritating behaviour as first one and then another went out as if they were snuffed by an invisible hand. But Dr

Kilner was not put off; as soon as he had Corder's skull he wired another spare anatomical skull in its place and made his escape before he was discovered!

He had his prize polished, mounted and installed in a square ebony box which he placed in a cabinet in his drawing room, but as he confided to Hopkins Senior, from the moment the skull was in his possession he felt uneasy about it. He was not the kind of man to imagine that the skull could be haunted. All that kind of thing was mumbo-jumbo in his opinion, and surely after so many years at the hospital being used by doctors and students, any supernatural influence must have disappeared long since.

A few days after the skull was installed at Dr Kilner's home his servant came to tell him that a gentleman had called to see him. The doctor was not pleased as it was after surgery hours, and when he asked her if the caller was a patient she recognised, she replied that she had never seen him before. 'He is proper old-fashioned looking,' she said, 'with a furry top hat and a blue overcoat with silver buttons.'

The doctor went to the surgery to see his visitor, asking the servant to bring a lamp as it was getting dark. As he looked into the room, he had the impression that there was someone standing by the window, but when the servant followed him in with the lamp, there was no one there.

The servant insisted that a gentleman had called and been shown into the surgery, but it looked as if he must have changed his mind and decided not to wait.

The doctor thought little of the incident, but one evening soon afterwards he was looking out of the window when he noticed a figure at the end of the lawn by the summerhouse. Someone who was wearing a beaver hat and an old-fashioned great coat! The doctor stepped out into the garden to accost the intruder, but before he could reach him, the figure vanished.

Dr Kilner found these two incidents disturbing, and during subsequent days he often had the uneasy sensation that someone was following him.

At night he sometimes heard doors opening and the sound of footsteps. Even worse was the heavy breathing and muttering outside bedroom doors, and sometimes the sound of hammering and sobbing coming from the drawing room below. And in his restless sleep there were dreams in which someone seemed to be pleading with him. In the end sleep became impossible and despite his usual dismissive and robust attitude to the supernatural, the doctor had no doubt that it was the skull in his drawing room that was the cause of what was happening.

It seemed obvious that the ghost of William Corder wanted his skull and skeleton to be reunited, but this was impossible. Now that the skull had been polished, the difference would immediately be noticed if he put it back. And he would have to admit that he, a respectable doctor, had taken it! It was a dreadful dilemma. One night he had scarcely fallen asleep before something woke him. It was a sound downstairs, and he listened for a moment or two before lighting a candle and quietly walking out onto the landing. Looking down over the stair-rail he could just see the glass handle of the drawing room door and as he looked a hand closed over it, although he could not see anyone, simply a disembodied hand. Then as he watched the door knob was slowly turned and quietly the door of the drawing room opened.

The doctor had been so absorbed in what was happening that he was almost startled out of his wits by what occurred next. There was a loud explosion, almost as if someone had fired a gun in the drawing room, and pausing only to grasp a heavy candlestick as a weapon, the doctor ran downstairs to the drawing room. But as he reached the door a tremendous gust of wind met him, blowing out his candle and enveloping him in what seemed like a malevolent force. He felt as if he was fighting his way into the room, where he struggled to strike a match to relight his candle.

Then as the light flickered over the room he saw that the box which held Corder's skull was shattered into minute fragments. The door to the cabinet where the box had been was open, and on the shelf stood the skull, grinning evilly.

Dr Kilner could not wait to get rid of it. In view of their friendship, it seems rather strange that he offered the skull to Hopkins Senior, who walked home with it wrapped in a silk handkerchief. On his way he twisted his foot and fell heavily on the steps of the Angel Hotel, just as a lady of his acquaintance was passing. As the skull rolled at her feet she screamed, staring at it in horror, then hurried by without a word. There was nothing that Hopkins Senior could say in explanation, and apparently the lady in question never referred to it afterwards.

The twisted foot kept Mr Hopkins in bed for a week, and shortly afterwards his best mare rolled into a chalk pit and broke her back. Illness, sorrow and financial disaster followed for both Hopkins and Kilner, leaving them almost bankrupt, and it was obvious that the skull's reign of terror had to be broken. Mr Hopkins' solution was to take it to a country churchyard not far from Bury St Edmunds and bribe a gravedigger to give it a Christian burial.

To everyone's relief this apparently broke the spell, and in due course peace and good fortune returned.

'You will say that this story is an invention,' wrote R. Thurston Hopkins in his book *Ghosts Over England*, published in 1953. 'But you will be greatly mistaken. Names, places and events are openly and correctly stated, and can be verified. So if ever you come across a tortoise-shell-tinted skull in a japanned cash box, leave it severely alone. If you take it home there will be the Devil to Pay – and you may not be prepared to meet his bill!'

The Haunt of the Black Dog

Most areas have their own particular ghost but there is one supernatural creature that knows no boundaries. The terror of the Black Dog spreads like a stain over much of the country although each area has its own name for the huge beast with glowing eyes which pads silently along lonely lanes, ancient tracks and coastal paths. Alarming as his appearance may be to a lone traveller, tradition has it that a sighting is also an omen of death and disaster to the terrified onlooker. But the number of witnesses who have encountered the devil dog and lived to tell the tale give the lie to this superstition.

In the North of England he is the Padfoot, Shriker or Trash, in Norfolk Black Shuck or the Snarleyow, and in Suffolk he is Shuck or the Galleytrot, whereas in Wales there is a whole pack of devil dogs, the Cwm Annum, the creatures of Annwn, King of the Underworld, said to be the souls of those doomed to wander for ever in purgatory. Seen alone there, he is the Gwyllgi, known as the dog of darkness.

Dartmoor, too, has its legendary pack of hellhounds which range that bleak wilderness, but it is believed to be during a holiday in Cromer that Conan Doyle got the inspiration for his Hound of the Baskervilles, when he first heard about Black Shuck.

East Anglia has many tales of the Black Dog and on stormy nights tough old fishermen would say that this is the kind of weather when he is likely to be abroad, his blood-chilling howl rising above the sound of the wind.

The Galleytrot is reputed to have been seen near Leiston church, in the large churchyard fringed by lime trees and filled with ancient gravestones green with lichen. But when I was there no black hound made an appearance, not even a friendly Labrador.

In the early 1900s, two aristocratic ladies, Lady Walsingham and Lady Rendlesham, once sat up one night in the churchyard hoping for a glimpse of the legendary hound. Sure enough, at midnight, they saw slinking between the gravestones a dark shadowy form which leapt over the churchyard wall and disappeared down the lane.

Ancient tracks are haunts of the Black Dog, and he is said to range along the Devil's Ditch, a defensive earthwork which peters out close to the village of Reach, just over the border in Cambridgeshire. It runs as far as Newmarket Heath, crossing the A11 and A14 north of the roundabout where the roads join.

In his *Ghost Book*, Alasdair Alpin MacGregor reports that one evening in the early autumn of 1938 an Aldeburgh man was on his way home from Bungay, walking towards Ditchingham station. He noticed a black object approaching, and as it got nearer he could see that it was a large black dog with a long shaggy coat. It was on the same side of the road and he moved into the centre of the road to let it pass, but as it drew level with him, it vanished! Naturally he recounted this extraordinary experience to his friends in the 'local', and was told that Black Shuck was known to frequent the neighbourhood and quite a number of people had seen him.

There have been other sightings too: near Reydon Hall, on the road between Middleton in Essex and Boxford in Suffolk, at Wicken Fen near Newmarket and on the Cromer to Aldeburgh coast road. MacGregor relates that one evening at the beginning of the 20th century a Southwold couple were driving home near Reydon Hall when Black Shuck appeared almost under the horses' hooves. But when the driver hit out at it with his whip to frighten it off, concerned that they might run over it, 'it just wasn't there any longer.'

But one of the most frigthening encounters happened during the last war. An American airman and his wife had rented a flat-topped hut on the edge of Walberswick Marsh while the husband was serving at the nearby airbase. One evening during a bad storm they suddenly heard loud pounding on the door, and when the airman looked through the window, he was amazed to see a huge black dog repeatedly hurling its body at their hut.

It must have seemed an incredible nightmare, but as it went on the couple piled whatever furniture they had against the door, becoming terrified as the creature still continued to batter the hut walls, and even jumped up onto the flat room.

Their ordeal continued for some hours, but as dawn arrived at last and the noise ceased, they cautiously emerged to inspect the damage. To their amazement there was no evidence of the ferocious battering of the night before, and no paw marks in the soft mud round the hut.

Alasdair Alpin MacGregor also described another Walberswick inhabitant's sighting of 'the terrible monster of the Common'. She and her sister-in-law saw 'a phantom dog the size of a calf' and said that on stormy nights it had often been both seen and heard on its travels between Aldeburgh and Cromer.

But the most unforgettable Black Dog case dates back many centuries to 4th August 1577 when 'a Straunge and terrible Wunder' befell the churches of Bungay and Blythburgh. During morning service at St Mary's church, Bungay, an unusually violent storm was raging outside when the service was disrupted as a huge black dog burst in surrounded by lightning flashes. It swept through the building 'with great swiftnesse and incredible haste among the people' and when it passed between two of the worshippers according to the old 16th century tract, it 'wrung the necks of them bothe at one instant clene backward insomuch that, even at a moment where they kneeled, they straungely died'. Another unfortunate man survived, but was shrivelled up 'like a piece of leather scorched in a hot fire'.

This creature, believed by the people to have been the Devil in the form of Black Shuck, also burst upon the congregation at Blythburgh church on the same day, killing two men and a young lad and leaving his trademark in the form of deep black marks, said to be claw marks, on the north door, which can still be seen. Bungay's memento is in the form of a Black Dog weathervane in the town centre.

As well as the Black Dog's fearsome appearance, people say there is a sulphurous smell and when places where it has appeared are examined, a smell of brimstone is noticed and the ground appears to be scorched. Small wonder then, that Black Dogs are believed to be creatures of the Devil, if not the Devil himself in the form of a dog.

Another supernatural creature with some resemblance to Black Shuck is known as the Shug Monkey, sometimes seen nearby in Cambridgeshire in a lane called Slough Hill on the road between West Wratting and Balsham. A witness described it as 'a cross between a big rough coated dog and a monkey with big shining eyes. Sometimes it would shuffle along on its hind legs and at other times it would whizz past on all fours.'

These days we hear more about sightings of large black cats than black dogs. There is something almost supernatural about those reported glimpses of an unusual beast spotted in the distance or appearing in the car headlights and vanishing just as suddenly. Could some of them have been our old friend Black Shuck? It's said he has his roots in the Hound of Odin whose Norse legend arrived on our shores with the Viking invasion. And certainly he is one of the oldest and most terrifying reported phantoms known in this country.

SURREY

The Death of Percy Lambert

'**H**ey, you, stop! Stop, I say!' yelled the security guard as the silent figure wandered off into the mist towards the river. But his words seemed not to penetrate the dank air. The guard walked quickly in the same direction, tracking the nocturnal trespasser, wondering what the man was doing here. A few yards further on and he could see the man no more. The dark figure had evaporated into the chill night air and vanished.

Who was he, this strange figure, so quaintly dressed in racing helmet and goggles? And where had he gone? In his heart the guard already knew the answer to the second question as he stood, shivering a little, peering into the foggy gloom beyond the aircraft factory buildings. The man he had seen was not of this world. He belonged to the unique history of this place and his name was Percy Lambert. This is his story.

The morning of Friday, 31st October 1913 dawned heavy with mist and dampness, but by 9 o'clock it had cleared and a fine autumn day was in prospect. Percy Lambert, or 'Pearly' as he was known, sat ready at the wheel of his streamlined 25 hp Talbot racing car on the start line of Surrey's 'eighth wonder of the world' – Brooklands.

Brooklands Motor Course was the brainchild of a single-minded man dedicated to the motorcar. His name was Hugh Locke King and he lived in a large house near Weybridge station on the edge of St George's Hill. For generations his family had owned estates around Weybridge and the surrounding country. He was an instantly recognisable figure as he drove about the district in his large 'Itala'. Sometimes he took the car on extensive Continental tours.

Locke King was particularly concerned that British car builders should

*Percy Lambert, who crashed while beating the land speed record at Brooklands
Motor Course in October 1913. (Inset) Margaret Morten, they were to
have been married two weeks later*

be given every facility to develop vehicles as good as their counterparts in
Europe. But, in the main, the British establishment was against the
'horseless carriage', limiting its speed on the open road to twenty miles
per hour. In towns it was half that speed, and many local magistrates
soon gained a reputation for the swingeing fines they imposed on those
who dared to use the full power of their motors. Some Surrey towns, such
as Godalming, were notorious among the motoring fraternity for the

efficiency of their speed traps. The motor industries in France and Italy faced no such restrictions. Locke King recognised that the country needed a purpose-built track on private land, where cars could be tested and raced flat out for hour after hour without their drivers facing arrest.

Below St George's Hill, the Locke King Estate included a large tract of damp and marshy meadowland astride the meandering river Wey. The place was infested with rabbits and not much else. Locke King was determined that this was the spot where his motor track would be built. In 1906 plans were drawn up, and in eight months the area transformed. It was a colossal undertaking.

Brooklands Motor Course was officially opened on 17th June 1907. In just a few short months peaceful meadow had been turned into two and three-quarter miles of oval, 100 foot wide, concrete track, with a separate finishing straight in the middle. This giant arena, with the spectacular banking of its bends, awaited the combat of its motorised gladiators.

However, the first meeting, held on 6th July 1907, was not a great success. The races were difficult to follow, mainly because the cars raced without numbers. Spectators were expected to identify them by means of the racing colours worn by the drivers, rather like jockeys. This similarity to horse racing extended to entry fees and prize money, which were given in sovereigns, while the results of each race were put up on a board just like those still seen today at Sandown, just a few miles from Brooklands. The official starter just happened to be a member of the Jockey Club. Modern motor racing tracks still have a paddock, but the first one was at Brooklands.

However, once the problems had been ironed out, the crowds began to flock to see this exciting new spectator sport. The track also became very popular with drivers and car makers seeking speed and endurance records. By October 1913, many of the drivers had become public heroes, none more so than the 32 year old record breaker, Percy Lambert.

The previous February he had become the first driver in the world to cover 100 miles in an hour. But now the record stood at 107.95 mph and was held by a Frenchman, Jean Chassagne, driving a Sunbeam. Percy Lambert was anxious to regain the record before the year was out.

Motor racing was his life, and he had been here many times before, feeling the tingling anticipation of the exhilaration ahead, resolute in his determination to beat the world record. Percy was a dedicated man – he always trained to peak fitness for his record attempts. He never drank alcohol and very seldom smoked. Since 7 o'clock that morning he had waited patiently for the sun to lift the clammy vapours of an October night. He was confident that his massive machine, with its 4,754 cc, four cylinder engine and weighing well over a ton, would soon regain the prize for his sponsor, Lord Shrewsbury.

Tyres were always a problem in the early days of speed. The technology of the pneumatic tyre had lagged behind the rapid progress made by engine designers. On the previous Monday Percy Lambert had been lucky when a tyre on his Talbot had burst. For this fresh attempt on the record a set of brand new Palmer cord tyres had been fitted to the steel rims on the wood-spoked wheels. As an extra special precaution, about a dozen security bolts were fixed to each of them to prevent any chance of the tyres moving on their rims. No detail had been left unconsidered – the car had been thoroughly checked in every detail. Percy and his mechanics were totally confident that the Frenchman's record would fall.

At 9.20 the Talbot scorched from the start line, the thump and thunder of its massive four cylinders soon blending into an ear-splitting roar, the helmeted driver, goggles down, hunched over the huge steering wheel.

All was going to plan – the Talbot hurtling round, high on the banking, with metronomic regularity. Among the spectators was William Macintyre, son of one of the Brooklands lodgekeepers, who had come to watch from the safety of the Members' Bridge. After about half an hour, the Talbot had completed twenty laps of the track at an average speed of 110.4 mph. A split second after disappearing from view behind Members' Hill, while three-quarters of the way round the twenty-first lap, there was a loud bang. The eerie silence that followed was long enough for Major

Lindsay Lloyd, Clerk of the Course, who was timing Lambert, to remark to a companion 'He has burst another tyre'. The silence was then broken by a 'horrible clatter', which told all those present that there had been a terrible accident.

Meanwhile, William Macintyre, from his vantage point on the bridge, had seen the fate of Percy Lambert unfold almost beneath his feet.

'As Mr Lambert came round the bend behind the hill, travelling to the top of the bank, one of his tyres burst,' Macintyre reported. 'He swerved half-way down the bank and then resumed a straight course at a somewhat reduced speed. The car travelled irregularly for about fifty yards, and then turned upwards and got on top of the bank, the off-side wheels going over the cement on to the sand on the other side.'

Macintyre was witnessing a driver struggling for his life, wrestling with a writhing monster on a wall of death.

'After travelling in this position a very little distance, the car turned turtle,' Macintyre continued. 'It then began to roll over and over down the cement.' Percy Lambert had lost the struggle.

'After the second roll I saw Mr Lambert lying on the track.'

Those who rushed to the scene found Percy Lambert lying face down about halfway up the banking. He was unconscious but still breathing. The car was standing upright against the brickwork of the bridge; the remains of the burst offside rear tyre were about ten or fifteen yards away. Percy Lambert was rushed to Weybridge Cottage Hospital in Brooklands' own ambulance, but all life was extinguished during the few minutes of the journey.

The mortal remains of Percy Lambert, who had lived in Knightsbridge, were buried in Brompton Cemetery, a spoked wheel marking his grave. It was suggested at the inquest on the day following his death that, had he succeeded in this record attempt, he intended to retire from record breaking. But records were Percy Lambert's goal in life and perhaps in death too, for it was not long before stories began to circulate of a ghostly figure, with racing helmet and goggles, seen walking along the track. There were reports also of the sound of the 25 hp Talbot as it roared invisibly around Brooklands' massive banking. It was even claimed that the car itself had been seen, Percy Lambert at the wheel. It travelled for about a hundred feet and then vanished.

The spot where Percy Lambert died by Members' Bridge is still recognisable today. That this place is haunted, there can be no doubt. Test Hill, a very steep incline once used for cars, motorcycles and even bicycles, runs up towards the track near the bridge. One night in the early 1970s a British Aircraft Corporation security man was looking across towards the hill, when he saw a large blob of 'blackness' floating above the area. Then he heard a terrible sound of 'crashing, splintering metal or wood. I was petrified to the extent that I could not move. Test Hill was still overgrown at that time, but two days later, when I plucked up courage to investigate, not a blade of grass, nor a branch of a tree had been broken,' he related sometime later.

'There is definitely something strange in that area, and I'm a level headed chap who doesn't imagine things,' he insisted.

Many people now agree that the haunting of that area must be related to the tragedy of an October day in 1913.

Following the First World War, Brooklands went from success to success, not just as a centre of motor racing, but also for motorcycles, bicycles and, of course, aircraft. In 1935 John Cobb in his giant 'Napier-Railton' with its 450 hp, 12 cylinder, aero engine, raised the lap record to a staggering 143.44 mph, a record which was never to be broken.

The onset of war in 1939 saw the end of racing at Brooklands as all activity was concentrated on aircraft production, which the great aviation pioneer A.V. Roe had initiated back in December 1907. During the war, hangars were built on the track and part of the embankment dug away. The story of the Brooklands Motor Course was at an end, but its heyday has not been forgotten.

Brooklands Museum, tracing all aspects of its unique history, has opened using the old clubhouse as its centre. Substantial parts of the famous banking have survived, and where Percy Lambert lost his life his spirit lingers, still seeking a record that is really his.

❖

Take Me Home

Many people experience at some time in their lives an incident which cannot be explained by normal criteria. Some quickly push such an occurrence to the back of their mind, thinking 'I must have been dreaming, or drinking,' and often there is a reluctance to tell others of their experience lest they should be considered odd. And yet they find it impossible to forget the haunting memory of something apparently unbelievable, because they know it really happened!

One dark, gloomy wet Saturday night in 1947 a man was driving home in his van along Portsmouth Road towards Cobham. It was well after 11 o'clock, and as he descended Tartar Hill he noticed a young girl at the side of the road, trying to wave him down. Normally he would not have stopped in these circumstances, but without thinking he found himself pulling to a halt outside the Tartar pub. He pushed open the door and silently she climbed in. She did not speak and neither did he.

The rain poured down like the tapping of a thousand fingers upon the van roof as he waited, but still nothing was said. The girl did not look at him but stared straight ahead, the faint light from the pub illuminating the pallor of her skin.

He started the engine and drove away down the hill towards Cobham. The girl was still looking ahead at the road glistening before them, her dark eyes blank and impenetrable, and a strange feeling akin to fear was starting in the pit of the man's stomach. The journey to the High Street seemed interminable but still the girl said nothing, and his uneasiness gave way to irritation. Why didn't she say where she wanted to go?

Assuming that she might want to get out there he drew up in the High Street, but his passenger still sat immobile, her hands in her lap. And he noticed for the first time how unusually grey her hair seemed for such a young girl.

For reasons he could not have explained, he found himself unable to ask her where she wanted to go, so he started his van again and headed for home, hoping that at some point his silent companion would somehow indicate her destination. He turned down Church Street just as the church clock was striking midnight and suddenly the engine cut out and the vehicle coasted slowly to a halt by the side of the churchyard.

Without a word the girl opened the door and got out. It was raining hard and she picked up the man's coat, putting it over her head as she ran off, and he watched her flitting through the churchyard in the direction of a house on the far side.

He was tempted to go after her, but found he could not move. His arms felt like lead. How long he stayed there like that he did not know, but eventually his hand moved to the ignition, the engine fired and the man drove slowly on his way.

Afterwards he could not bring himself to mention this strange incident to either family or friends. Then about a week later while going about his normal business, he found himself driving once more down Church Street, Cobham. Curiosity got the better of him, so he parked his van and threaded his way through the churchyard towards the house he presumed the girl had been making for. The door was opened by a smart, well-dressed man with a pleasant face, but the sharp lines round his mouth and eyes told of past tragedies.

'I have come to collect my coat. I think it was your daughter who borrowed it from me last week.'

The man smiled gently. 'So you've seen her too? You're not the first.'

He paused, then continued. 'My daughter died in a fire in this house ten years ago. She had been out with friends, to the Tartar pub I believe.

She came home later than she should have. It was the time we had the electricians here and that night we had no power, so she took a candle up to her bedroom. She must have been reading in bed and fallen asleep. Something must have knocked the candle over. It was the smoke that killed her.'

The driver mumbled something about how sorry he was.

'Let me take you to her grave. We had her buried just over there so she would still be near us.'

The van driver followed the father back through the gravestones until they came to a well-kept grave, ablaze with flowers. Somehow it was no surprise to find his coat lying on the gravestone.

Just then a breeze got up, murmuring in the trees. The driver could hear the church clock striking and could once again see the wet road stretching before him. Something touched his arm, and a quiet voice seemed to say: 'Thank you for taking me home.'

SUSSEX

The Girl with Golden Ringlets

T wo of the most evocative place names in Sussex are surely Amberley and the Wild Brooks. The Wild Brooks are in fact marshland liable to flooding at times from the river Arun. The church at Amberley is cheek by jowl with the castle which was once the favourite residence of the Bishops of Chichester. Naturally the church needed a vicarage to house a priest to minister to the people in the thatched cottages. It is this vicarage which is haunted.

The vicarage has cellars dating back to Elizabethan times but the house itself was completely rebuilt in the 1720s when Bell Carelton was the vicar. Even then it was only a one-storey building with a thatched roof and a verandah on the west side. It did not gain another storey until the late 1890s when the Rev William Streatfield was vicar. He and hs famly moved to Amberley in 1897 when his second daughter was two years old. Her name was Noel Streatfield, later to become a prolific writer and one of whose best loved books is *Ballet Shoes*.

Noel often played alone at Amberley after her adored elder sister Ruth had to be sent away because the dampness of the place affected her delicate health. Noel had a young brother and sister but they preferred each other's company. So Noel frequently amused herself in the garden. There was a mulberry tree and a hornbeam, but best of all, away from the house, there was an unusual rose tree which had flowers half white and half red and so was called a 'York and Lancaster'.

Noel adopted the rose tree as her own special possession but gradually she came to realise there was another little girl who also loved the rose tree. This little girl wore long white pantalettes and a crinoline. Her golden hair was parted in the middle and fell in ringlets on either side.

Noel Streatfield, who once had a ghostly friend at Amberley Vicarage

Noel accepted her quite naturally and she did not feel any surprise at her presence although she only saw her in the garden. But the little girl was heard in the house quite often. She was inquisitive and liked to inspect new guests. When visitors came to stay at the vicarage, the handle would turn and the door of the spare room would open while footsteps pattered lightly over the floor. Visitors found this unnerving and one left hurriedly, even before breakfast!

There was a conspiracy of silence about the ghost because the servants knew and never mentioned it to the family while Noel never dreamed of telling her parents.

It is strange how the villagers also chose to remain silent about the ghost. It is possible they thought the vicar would be sceptical about such things or perhaps they feared he and his family would be frightened into leaving. Thus silence becomes a tradition.

In 1902 the Rev W. Streatfield left to become vicar of St Peter's church at St Leonards and the new incumbent at Amberley was the Rev Dr G. F. Carr who arrived with his family. Mrs Carr saw the little girl and she was so clear and lifelike that Mrs Carr could not beleive she was not a real child. She saw her through the dining-room window one afternoon and she watched her walk up the garden path towards the house. Mrs Carr noted too the white dress and fair curls and she thought the child was about seven years old. Mrs Carr waited for her to ring the front door bell and when nothing happened she went to ask the servants what had become of the child but they had seen nothing at all untoward.

There is a last satisfying footnote to this Amberley ghost. In 1904 the Carrs decided the vicarage must be renovated and an old wall was demolished so that the dining-room could be enlarged. While digging out the foundations, the workmen came upon a trench which contained earth of a different colour to the sourrounding area. At about two feet below the surface which had once been covered by the old floorboards in the corner of the dining-room, the workmen discovered two skeletons, one of a woman and the other belonging to a child of about seven years of age. It was remembered then how the Rev George Arthur Clarkson, the vicar before the Streatfields and who had lived at Amberley for almost 50 years, had often complained about a bad smell in the dining-room. But nothing was ever done about it perhaps because it was put down to country drains.

The bones were buried in consecrated ground but not before several pieces had been carried off by the villagers as souvenirs. All the same the ghost of the little girl has not been seen again so it seems that she has found peace at last.

❖

Mysterious Music

George Aitchison, journalist and author of *Unknown Brighton*, was of the opionion that ghostly sounds are the last vestiges of a haunting. By inference it follows that soon there would be nothing left at all. However, it may be that mysterious music comes in a category of its own and is not dependent on other ghostly manifestations.

One of the best documented cases of supernatural music relates to the chanting monks of Poling. Martha Bates, who was born in 1870, had always been interested in ghosts. Perhaps it ran in the family because as a small child she had listened to her grandfather's stories of Sussex ghosts. Although these were told on dark evenings in the winter beside a flickering fire, she seems to have been enthralled rather than frightened. When she became a young lady with her hair swept up and wore the long sleeved and high necked dresses of the period, she began keeping a journal of her ghostly experiences.

She had heard about the monks at Poling and nothing would satisfy her except hearing the chanting for herself. She obtained permission from the owner of the house and she persuaded a relative to accompany her. Her companion was most carefully chosen because he was a professor of music and she judged that he would be able to identify any obscure music they might hear. He must have been a patient man or perhaps young Martha had infected him with some of her enthusiasm. At any rate they spent six long nights in fruitless vigil. On the last night they were sitting in a corridor in the oldest part of the house, huddled in blankets to try to keep warm, when they heard the chanting. It started off softly as though in the distance and then became louder as though a procession of monks were walking invisibly past them and the chanting faded away on the other side. The professor had no hesitation in stating that the music was a Gregorian funeral chant.

Confirmation of the phenomenon is provided by Philip M. Johnstone whose brother Sir Harry Hamilton Johnstone (1858–1927) owned the old farmhouse at Poling. Philip was an authority on Sussex churches and it was he who heard the chanting on several occasions when he went to stay with his brother. At first Philip was too surprised to register anything except the unexpectedness of the chanting. But as he became more familiar with the experience, he noticed that the chant was always the same. He was able to write down the notes he heard and he sent the score to a friend who knew about ancient music. The friend identified it as a Gregorian setting of the *Deus Misereatur* (the 67th Psalm) used at funerals. Philip Johnstone told the story to George Aitchison and to Arthur Beckett, author and editor of the *Sussex County Magazine* and they both had no doubts about accepting the truth of it.

The church of St Andrew, Didling (south-west of Midhurst) is small and stands by itself and is much praised for the antiquity and solidity of its pews. In the 1940s it became noted for something else – its ghostly choir. What is particularly interesting is that eyewitness accounts differ as to whether it was a single voice or a choir.

In the autumn of 1926 Z.A. Tickner went to visit friends who had recently moved house. He had never been to Didling before so he decided to explore. He walked around the farm and on being told where he could find the key, he decided to look inside the church. It was midday and the sun was shining. There was no sound from either farm machinery or traffic in the lane. Yet as he pushed open the door he distinctly heard the sound of men's voices singing plainsong. He looked again outside the church but nothing stirred and when he entered the church the singing had stopped. He searched inside the little church, even peeping behind the curtain but there was nobody there. He then went back and swung the door on its hinge but there was no sound of creaking. He never told anyone about his experience until years later.

On the other hand the late Rev W.W. Whistler was certain that the ghost voice was a single, very pure soprano. He was taking an afternoon service one Sunday and his congregation consisted of a handful of worshippers, all adult and some elderly. He was greatly astonished when he heard this pure voice singing in tune with the hymn and he knew that none of his flock could sing like that. He heard it two or three times singing a line or two of the hymn and then fading. The lady organist was delighted when he told her because she had heard the voice on several occasions and she had not liked to mention it before.

This story was printed in the *Sussex County Magazine* in 1943 and it soon prompted Z.A. Tickner to write in and tell about his experience there.

Unexplained music of a secular sort has been heard at Yapton. A recently retired man of 60 accompanied by his elderly parents had taken up temporary residence at Yapton while he searched for a suitable plot of ground on which to build a bungalow. One evening in the spring of 1956 two days after his arrival at Yapton, he was taking a stroll at about 9.30 pm. It was a peaceful walk beside the old elms and high wall with here and there a cottage. He was surprisd to hear the unmistakable sound of a lively polka being played on a quartet of stringed instruments. He felt sure a party was in progress and that when he rounded the corner he would see a big house alive with lights and the noise of people within. But all he found was an ordinary cottage with no brilliant lights. He stood there for about 10 minutes listening to the polka music, imagining that perhaps the party was being held at the back out of sight. It puzzled him that only the polka was played and no other sort of dance. He also found it strange that when he had moved several hundred yards from the cottage, he could still hear the polka as clearly as when he had been standing outside.

He went to bed just after midnight and he dreamed he heard the polka being played twice over on a single violin. Strange to relate, the following morning his parents said to him that he ought not to play his gramophone so late at night. They too had heard the polka played twice over. But the man did not own such a record and besides his record player was still packed up and there were no power points in the bedroom.

The only likely explanation is that music from a long ago party came through that night for some reason. The polka was a Bohemian dance which originated in about 1830. When it was introduced into this country it became a sensation. No doubt the older folk disapproved mightily and thought it the height of decadence while for younger people a party with polka after polka would have been very popular.

TYNE & WEAR

The Cauld Lad of Hylton Castle

The ghost of ancient Hylton Castle, which goes by the name of the Cauld Lad, seems to be a dual personality. The old story concerns a brownie, one of those useful, but often tricky, characters from the realm of faery, who delighted in performing a range of useful domestic tasks overnight. But if the servants had left everything in good order with nothing for him to do, the Cauld Lad was outraged to find his work done, and would go on the rampage, creating mayhem everywhere.

So his activities as a home help were something of a mixed blessing, and someone remembered that, according to legend, the way to send a troublesome brownie on his way was to present him with some clothes. And so a suit, cloak and hood were made in the Cauld Lad's size and left out for him to find. At midnight as usual he appeared, and immediately noticed the handsome green outfit waiting there. Of course he couldn't resist trying it on, and parading proudly round the kitchen admiring himself. But as daylight approached, he stopped, and with the words 'Here's a cloak and here's a hood, the Cauld Lad of Hylton will do no more good', he was gone, never to return.

However, Hylton's other ghost was no brownie, but a young stable lad who, in the early 17th century, was sent by his master, Robert Hylton, to fetch his horse. But the lad was so long returning that Hylton went in search and found him asleep in the stable. This so angered him that he hit out at the boy with a pitchfork, and killed him, later hiding the body by throwing it into a pond. Years later his skeleton was found, and somehow the ghost of the stable boy and the brownie have become confused as Hylton Castle's famous Cauld Lad.

WARWICKSHIRE

The Battle in the Skies

E dgehill is reputed to be the most haunted battlefield in England, and a recital of the extraordinary phenomena witnessed here from time to time would fill an entire book on its own! For many years, on Edgehill Night, 23rd October, ghost hunters, serious and sceptical alike, have taken up positions on the hillside overlooking the plain, hoping that the strange manifestations would once again appear before them, but without success. Perhaps they should have remembered that the calendar has changed since 1642 and twelve days were 'lost'.

Edgehill was the first battle of the English Civil War; the first time King Charles I and the Parliament, with their opposing forces, met face to face. The battle began with a single musket shot fired in anger early on the morning of that bitterly cold 23rd October, and raged throughout the day. Many were valiant deeds and acts of great courage and bravery carried out by men on both sides, and the fighting was as bitter as the wind that blew across that flat land. As night began to close in, both sides fell back, leaving the field littered with dead and wounded. Reports of the number of dead vary enormously, between 1,500 and 6,000, and it is believed that many wounded were saved by the extreme cold of the night which lowered their body temperature and stopped them from bleeding to death.

The battle was by no means conclusive; neither side 'won'. The Roundheads fell back to the village of Kineton, where they found shelter and 'borrowed' or stole food and fodder. The King's forces moved off towards the town of Banbury.

The local inhabitants, simple peasants for the most part, had gazed in wonder at the sight of armed men, cannon and ordnance, and had

The Battle of Edgehill was re-enacted in the skies two months later

probably heaved a great sigh of relief when they all moved off. The whole event which had, for a few days, disrupted their particular bit of countryside could now be pushed to the back of their minds as they got on with the chores of their simple living, when suddenly they were once again plunged into the depths of fear.

One Saturday night, just before Christmas of that year, three shepherds walked together from their homes in Kineton to check on their flocks grazing near the site of the battle. They are described as 'poor ignorant men' who probably had no thought in their heads at this time other than the welfare of their sheep and how quickly they could get back home in the warm.

As they approached Edgehill field, they were halted by the sound of a great noise, and a light in the sky so bright it dazzled them. They were terrified, and amid the torn and crumpled turf where Englishmen had so lately fought and killed each other, they stood rooted to the spot, gazing upwards. Within the circle of great light, in the darkened skies above them, they watched the battle being re-enacted. They could not tear their gaze from it, and so real was it that they saw faces, heard the thunder of horses' hoofs, the cries of command. They shuddered to the roar of the cannon, and about their heads they felt the whistle of air from flying musket balls. With increasing horror, they listened to the screams of the dying and the groans of the wounded; the distant sound of the cornet and muffled drum beat, and the harsh sound of steel meeting steel from clashing sabres.

This continued unabated for three hours, during which time the three shepherds were completely unable to move, and all the while, in their fear, they thought their last hour on earth had come upon them.

The great light eventually died from the skies and the images faded. Only then were they able to force their legs to move, and to run as fast as they could back into Kineton to tell their story. Despite the lateness of the hour, they knocked upon the doors of the Minister, Mr Samuel Marshall, and a local Justice, Mr William Wood. These two august gentlemen heard the shepherds' tale with some scepticism, but on the following night, accompanied by a few other local notables, they went themselves to the battlefield. The same ghostly re-enactment occurred all over again, exactly as the shepherds had described it, and the entire party fled homewards.

For several night the spectral tumult was witnessed by many people, and the whole area was in a state of abject terror. We are told people hid themselves; others lay 'sweating halfe smothered in their beds...' Many women miscarried, and stout hearted men confessed their fear of death. So great was this fear that Samuel Marshall and William Wood set off for Oxford to seek audience with the King and apprise him of the strange circumstances.

The King, upon hearing the sorry tale, immediately sent Colonel Lewis Kirke and Captains Dudley and Wainman, together with three others, to see just what was afoot. They were not disappointed, for they too witnessed the ghostly battle in the skies. They, who had seen the reality on 23rd October, saw it all again, exactly as it had happened. They heard the sounds and cries, and they saw the faces of their dead comrades. They returned immediately and reported the truth of the story to the King.

It had been suggested that these manifestations might have been caused by some of the dead remaining on the field unburied, hidden from view amid furze and vegetation. Accordingly a search was made, and true enough, some bodies were found. These were given a proper and reverent Christian burial, and everyone hoped this would put an end to the terror engulfing them. But it was not to be. The great light – and the ghost battle – continued for some time until it eventually faded out.

Shortly afterwards, a pamphlet entitled *The New Yeare's Wonder* was issued by a London printer, Mr Thomas Jackson, who gave a colourful and exact description of the occurrences. It sold well!

Among those who lost their lives at Edgchill was Royalist Henry Kingsmill, from Hampshire. He too left a legend to linger after him. He rode into the battle on a great white horse, and it is this loyal creature which still remains, wandering riderless and unchecked, looking for its late master. The sound of ghostly hooves may be heard on 23rd October, when its great white misty shape looms out of the darkness, before it turns again on its eternal search.

Kingsmill was buried at nearby Radway, and some time after the end of the hostilities, his mother, Lady Bridget Kingsmill, caused an effigy to be erected to the memory of her brave son. Time and weather have not dealt kindly with this stone figure, but after 350 years it still remains. Legend has it that upon the anniversary of the battle, a small posy of flowers is found upon it. Who so honours the memory of Henry Kingsmill is not known.

Also legendary is the tale of the bloodstained barn, now long gone, where a wounded Royalist is supposed to have taken refuge. The blood that stained its wooden walls ran afresh every 23rd October.

Local land names bear witness to this past event. Graveground Coppice is where many of the dead were hurriedly interred in a mass grave, and where it is said local dogs and horses refuse to venture. Red

Road, a mere bridle track now, is supposed to have once run red with the blood of the wounded, escaping from the conflict. On 23rd October, in the dead of the night, legend has it you can still hear the shuffle of their booted feet as they limpingly make their way to safety.

There are quite a lot of ghosts left over from the Battle of Edgehill, quite apart from the manifestations on the actual battlefield. At Lighthorne and at Leek Wootton there are wraiths of young women weeping and wailing, thought to be the wives, now widows, of soldiers who died.

Middleton Hall, on the Northamptonshire side of the county, has the ghost of an Edgehill messenger. Legend has it that the man rode frantically, whipping his horse into a great lather, to bring news of the battle to the Willoughby family at the Hall. Crossing the drawbridge, the weary horse slipped and both man and horse drowned in the deep moat below. When the moat was filled in, in 1869, bones were found which lend credibility to this story.

At Warmington it is recorded that many of those wounded at Edgehill sought sanctuary there, mostly to die of their injuries. The vicar recorded the burial of one, Alexander Gourdin, who has a small headstone to mark his last resting place; he also recorded having buried seven more whose names he did not know, and that many others were buried 'in the fields and wynds of Warmington' where they fell. They do say that sometimes, at night, you can still hear cries of pain from those who came to Warmington to die.

It is no longer possible to venture anywhere near the site of this famous battle. The entire area was taken over by army authorities some years ago, and there is now tight security. But thereby hangs another tale.

WILTSHIRE

The Legend of Littlecote House

L ittlecote House is a splendid mansion which lies between Marlborough in Wiltshire and Hungerford in Berkshire. It was built around 1500 by the Darrell family whose name will ever be associated with its notorious member, known as Wild William Darrell, and his barbaric crime. It was a dark and stormy night in 1575 when some men arrived at the home of Mother Barnes, a midwife in the nearby village of Great Shefford to request her urgent help for a lady in labour. When she agreed, she was blindfolded and taken pillion on horseback to a splendid mansion where the door was opened by a tall man holding a light, who hurriedly closed the door behind her and took her upstairs. They passed through a room where a huge fire was burning into a bed chamber where there was a four-poster bed with the curtains drawn.

According to Mother Barnes' own account later, the man whispered to her that the gentlewoman who needed her services was in the bed, and if she was safely delivered of her child, the midwife would be well rewarded, but 'if she miscarry in her labour, you shall die'. One can imagine the midwife's state of mind as she drew back the bed curtains and found a young woman there, her face masked, in the final stages of childbirth.

A male baby was born soon afterwards and having nothing better to wrap him in, the midwife used her own apron. As she left the bedroom to ask for some clothing for the child she was met by the nobleman who had let her in, who asked if the lady had given birth. When Mother Barnes showed him the baby, he demanded that she throw it into the fire. Horrified she pleaded with him, even offering to take the child away and bring it up as her own, but the man snatched the baby from her and threw it into the fire, ordering the distressed midwife back to the bedroom to take care of the woman there. This she did, but had the

Littlecote House, the home of Wild Will Darrell – and several ghosts

presence of mind to snip a small piece from the bed curtain, and when eventually she was allowed to return home, she also counted the stairs down to the hall, to help identify the mansion.

Later the midwife reported what had happened to the local magistrate, and her evidence and the piece of material cut from the bed curtain identified Littlecote as the mansion, and William Darrell as the murderer, which in view of his debauched reputation caused no surprise locally. He was arrested and tried, but to the shocked surprise of the public, he was acquitted, after supposedly bribing the judge, Sir John Popham.

However, nemesis overtook Wild Will Darrell when he was out hunting one day in 1589 and as he approached a stile his horse shied and threw him, frightened by the ghost of the Burning Babe. Darrell broke his neck. The stile where it happened is known as Darrell's Stile and is said to be haunted by the ghost of Wild Will himself.

Littlecote is haunted by other ghosts such as a sad lady carrying a baby, who, if she is the mother of the murdered infant, is still unidentified. Rumour locally believed that she was Darrell's sister, and among other suggestions John Aubrey in his *Brief Lives* says she was Darrell's wife's maid but this would hardly have justified the heavy secrecy and Darrell's behaviour on the night of the murder.

But whoever the tragic mother was, she still haunts Littlecote where the ghosts also include a lady in a pink gown carrying a rushlight, a woman in flowing robes walking in the garden, and a man called Gerald

Lee Bevin, a tenant there in the 1920s who was sent to prison for a famous City swindle, and now haunts the Long Gallery.

When the mansion was in the possession of the Wills tobacco family, the owner's brother, Sir Edward Wills, and his wife were staying there in the winter of 1927. They were in a room a few steps up from the Long Gallery, and for two nights running they heard the creaking of the stairs as if someone was coming up, but as there was a nearby bathroom they thought little of it. But when it happened again Sir Edward opened his bedroom door and looked out. He saw a fair haired lady in a pink gown holding a light in her hand entering the dressing room where his brother was sleeping. He followed and found the room empty, except for his sleeping brother.

Peter de Savary bought Littlecote in 1985 and afterwards there was a sale of some of the effects of the previous owner. Later, in October 1993 de Savary told *Hello* magazine that on the morning of the sale he was in the garden when he met a lady dressed 'just like a lady you would find in Hungerford doing her shopping', in a tweed skirt and sweater. To his surprise she accosted him, saying he was a wicked man, and when he asked why, she said, 'You have taken my baby's things.' When, puzzled and anxious to help, he questioned her further, she explained about the clothes and where they should be, and thanks to his efforts the missing baby clothes were found, with a sketch of a baby's face and the words 'Early in the morning of Friday, June 21st 1861. Calm and cold – oh, so beautiful'. Another note had slits to hold the stems of flowers and the words 'Gathered at baby's grave, July 23rd 1861'. These items obviously relating to the tragic loss of a child were replaced as the ghost had wanted, and in the Littlecote chapel is the cast of a sleeping baby, the memorial which the grieving mother had sketched.

Thanks to Peter de Savary's kindness one ghost's mind was put at rest, but his description of her clothes is rather puzzling for a lady of the 19th century. Was his memory a little confused when he described her some years later, or after a few hundred years in the same old outfit, perhaps a fashion-conscious phantom may have decided to move with the times?

WORCESTERSHIRE

Priors Court, Callow End

Priors Court is a gabled, black and white timbered building a few miles south of Worcester, built in Elizabethan times on the site of a 13th century priory, and claims several ghosts from different periods of its history.

The wraith of one unfortunate lady dates back to the times when a priory stood there, and the tradition is that she was sheltering from a thunderstorm when some of the monks raped and murdered her, and threw her body into the river Severn. She is said to have been glimpsed several times in recent years.

The ghost of a Cavalier has been seen in the house and is believed to be connected with the skeleton found in one of the chimneys when some building work was being done. He may have been one of King Charles's companions who hid in the house after the Battle of Naseby.

A more charming ghost seen walking through the courtyard towards the orchard is a young Victorian girl, her hair drawn black in a bun beneath her straw hat. Is she the youthful member of the family who committed suicide after being crossed in love?

There is an interesting document of 1906 written by a Mrs. Abbott, who stayed at Priors Court on her honeymoon. She paid little heed to owner Lady Beauchamp's warning that the house was haunted, but in the early hours of July 14th suddenly awoke in a cold perspiration with the impression that there was someone by her bed.

She dismissed it as imagination when nothing else happened, but the following evening when she came out onto the landing she distinctly saw 'the figure of a woman dressed in an Empire gown'. She screamed, and

Are there secrets still to be discovered at Priors Court?

told one of the maids about it, but the maid laughed in disbelief. However, later that night when Mrs. Abbott was sitting in the kitchen with other people, she suddenly felt very cold, and saw the same apparition which lifted its arm and pointed to the garden with the words 'Garden, money, woman, brick' and disappeared. Mrs. Abbott was so frightened that she lost consciousness, but when she recovered the other people with her in the kitchen said that although they had seen her get up and speak they had seen nothing else.

A few evenings later she was upstairs and once again noticed that the air had become unusually cold, and saw the same figure again. It smiled at her and then 'glided away'.

A Mrs. Archdale rented Priors Court in 1906 and she, too, was told by Lady Beauchamp that several people had seen the ghost of a 'gentle looking lady in grey' walking around the house, and locally it was believed that it was one of two sisters who had quarrelled about some 'treasure' and one had murdered the other. After moving in both Mrs. Archdale and her husband sometimes noticed a sound like the steady rustling of a silk dress, which they could not account for. And one night after he had gone up to bed, her eldest son, then 14, was heard screaming with fright, and he said he had seen the ghost of a man in his bedroom.

Mrs. Archdale decided to have the house exorcised which seemed to have been successful at the time...

But the history of Priors Court has apparently left behind some echoes of its past. Books on black magic have been discovered in the attic, and human bones have been unearthed in the garden. Perhaps there are secrets yet to be discovered.

❖

A Grey Lady at Ye Olde Seven Stars Pub

Ye Olde Seven Starts pub is the venue where customers of Alan Lauder's Kidderminster Ghost Tours meet, an ideal place since it claims to be one of the most haunted hostelries in England.

The ghost is said to be a mysterious lady called Maggie Morgan. No one seems to know much about her, but she is capable of making her presence felt, and the dog is scared stiff when she is about!

One of the most haunted pubs in England – Ye Olde Seven Stars at Kidderminster

It was in 1974 that Maggie first got herself noticed. Mrs. Freda Holloway was serving in the bar one evening when she thought someone called her name, and she noticed a middle-aged woman standing at the end of the bar, wearing a white dress which she described as 'the kind worn at the turn of the century'. Then, said Freda, 'As I looked at her, the lady vanished.'

Mrs. Holloway saw the same phantom again on two separate occasions, and after a report appeared in the local press a reader wrote to the newspaper to say that his mother had been born in Ye Olde Seven Stars some 60 years earlier, and she too had seen the same apparition which she described as wearing a large old-fashioned white apron, not a white dress.

During 1974 two customers also saw the ghost at the bar, but only for a brief half minute or so before she simply faded away.

In 1989 Gary, a bartender, and another man who worked in the pub were painting the cellar when out of the corner of his eye Gary noticed that someone had come in. He just kept on painting as different people from the pub often looked in to see how they were getting on, but when no one spoke he turned round and saw something strange. He described it as the silhouette of a woman which seemed to be filled with smoke as he could see through it.

He and his companion simply stared at this apparition in astonishment. 'Then we looked at each other, and when we looked back at the silhouette it had gone,' he said. They ran upstairs to tell the licensee, who notified the local paper and gave them each a fiver for seeing the ghost!

Alan Lauder, who runs the Kidderminster Ghost Walks was in the pub with his wife and daughter one evening when they noticed a passer-by looking through the window at them. His young daughter joked that the man was admiring her because she was so pretty, to which Alan replied, 'I expect he thinks you are the Grey Lady.'

At that the bell at the bar began ringing very loudly which summoned the barman keen to know who was making such a din. Of course, Alan and his family were innocent! It was, they decided, another of the Grey Lady's little tricks.

YORKSHIRE

Close Encounters of a Deadly Kind

A t 3.30 pm on the sunny afternoon of Friday 6th June 1980, Zigmund Adamski set off from his home in Wakefield to the local shops – and vanished off the face of the earth. That was the last time anyone saw him alive, for his body was found in a coal hopper, five days after and 25 miles away in the market town of Todmorden.

How he got there, how he died, where he had been in the missing days, baffled everyone who investigated the mystery – and it remains unsolved to this day. In fact, there are those who believe it will never be explained – at least not in so-called 'rational' terms. However, to examine this mystery we must first look at the events leading up to the disappearance.

Zigmund Jan Adamski was Polish by birth and, like so many of his fellow countrymen, he had settled in England having been forced to flee his country during the war. He set up home in the West Yorkshire village of Tingley, became a coal miner and, in 1951, married Leokadia or 'Lottie'. When she became so ill that she was confined to a wheelchair, Zigmund needed to spend more time with her. His own health, too, was under question, and he had been off work for several months; a lung deformity often made breathing difficult – and it was with this extra factor that Zigmund decided to apply for early retirement. This was rejected, but his company's decision was reviewed quite soon after and the application subsequently accepted. Unfortunately, the reversed decision arrived in the post that day after he disappeared.

Upsetting though this was, family and friends were sure he had not gone missing through depression. He would never have left his wife; neighbours spoke of how devoted the couple were to each other.

On the day that Adamski disappeared, he had been shopping in Wakefield town centre with his cousin and her son who were visiting the Adamskis from Poland. That afternoon, the trio returned to the couple's home and sat down to a fish and chip dinner. Adamski was enjoying his cousin's visit and was also very excited about the next day; he was due to give away his god-daughter in marriage. He had a speech specially prepared for the occasion, and would not have let the couple down for any reason.

At half-past three, Adamski announced that he would pop out to the local shop just a few hundred yards down the street to buy some potatoes. He grabbed his jacket containing wallet, driving licence and some small change, and left the house. Passing a few desultory comments with a neighbour washing his car, he set off to the shops – but never reached them.

When Adamski did not return home that evening, Lottie contacted Wakefield police to report his disappearance, but despite intensive police enquiries and an appeal in local newspapers, their investigations drew a blank. That is, until almost exactly five days later to the minute, when his body was discovered.

At 3.45 pm, on Wednesday 11th June 1980, Trevor Parker, the son of a Todmorden coal merchant, arrived at his father's yard to find a man's body resting in a hollow at the top of a pile of coal. He had already been there that morning at 8.15 and was quite sure that the body was not there at that time. In the intervening hours, while Mr Parker had been absent, the gates of the yard had been left unlocked just in case any deliveries arrived. As it happens there had been none.

Mr Parker was understandably astonished to find the body, and he stood rooted to the spot for a while before composing himself and phoning for an ambulance. It was not only the fact that he had found the man here at all that was odd, for there were several other unaccountable points. It would have been a difficult task for a man to climb up the greasy side of the coal pile, even more so because it had been raining for most of the day, and Zigmund would have found it almost impossible because of his breathing problems. The dead man was wearing his jacket, but his shirt was missing; and Mr Parker had noticed a strange burn mark on the back of the man's head, neck and shoulder, which he would not touch.

Twenty-five minutes later, police officers Mervyn Haig and Alan Godfrey arrived to inspect the body and to question Mr Parker. The latter told them what he knew, but there seemed to be nothing which could throw light on the mystery. The body was transferred to the mortuary at nearby Hebden Bridge and, that night at 9.15 pm, a post-mortem was conducted by a consultant pathologist, to ascertain the cause of death.

From his examination, Dr Alan Edwards estimated that the time of death was between 11.15 am to 1.15 pm – around eight to ten hours prior to the post-mortem. The body, therefore, had been in the yard for at least two and a half hours before its discovery. No major physical injuries were evident – certainly no internal injuries – which showed he had probably not died from an assault of any kind. There were, however, the curious oval-shaped burn marks on the left of the neck and also below the ear. These had caused a slight loss of skin, brown discolouration and a tacky substance had been applied to them, presumably a form of ointment. Dr Edwards thought that the marks indicated contact with a corrosive substance but he could not ascertain what it was. Although the burns were not minor injuries he was sure they were not the cause of death. They could have caused some alarm to Adamski and brought on a heart attack. The final verdict was 'natural causes', as he had obviously died from heart and chest disease.

Even though Zigmund Adamski was found minus his shirt (which was never recovered) he had not been sleeping rough. His body showed that he had only one day's growth of stubble – so he had evidently been staying somewhere and, even though his stomach was empty, this merely indicated that he had not eaten on the day of his death. Dr Edwards found an abrasion on the man's thigh, and superficial cuts on both of his hands and knees.

UFOlogist Jenny Randles, who has written more than 20 books on

UFOs and the paranormal, including the *Pennine UFO Mystery*, points out that everyone who has investigated the case remains quite baffled.

The *Pennine UFO Mystery* is a down-to-earth investigation about a number of separate events that mainly occurred between June and November 1980, which the media linked together in a fantastic 'UFO' story. While Mrs Randles does not for one minute suggest that UFOs were responsible for the disappearance and subsequent reappearance and death of Zigmund Adamski, she does not dismiss the idea, either, sensibly leaving the reader to decide. While the UFO theory seems wildly improbable, it is pertinent, I think, to include the reasons why the Adamski death was initially linked to this phenomenon.

In the weeks leading up to the disappearance, there had been numerous reports to newspapers and the police about orange fireballs and other unidentified flying objects seen across West Yorkshire, mainly in Bradford, Halifax and Todmorden. While some of these sightings were explained away as aircraft, atmospheric phenomena, and flares used by moorland rescue teams, some remained unexplained, including quite a substantial amount which were reported *after* Adamski had disappeared.

In addition, one of the two police officers who arrived at the coalyard on 11th June allegedly had a close encounter with a UFO.

During the early morning of Friday 28th November 1980, policeman Alan Godfrey, who was on night patrol, was driving along Burnley Road, which leads out of Todmorden, when he saw a huge object with a spinning top section and a row of windows, hovering above the road ahead of him. He stopped the car 100 yards away from the UFO and attempted to contact the police station on both his car radio and mobile 'walkie-talkie', but he could not get through. The next thing he knew, he was 100 yards further down the road from where he had been and, although he didn't realise it at that moment, there had been a substantial time-lapse. Eventually, with advice from MUFORA (the Manchester UFO Research Association) he agreed to be hypnotised to discover what had happened during that missing time, of which he had no recollection. The subsequent hypnosis session brought to light PC Godfrey's astounding account of being taken inside the UFO and examined by alien beings, which seemed to have been buried in his subconscious and erased from conscious memory.

Whether or not this has any connection with the Adamski death is not known, but all investigators have been unable to find a conventional solution to the mystery. There are several reasons why Adamski was connected to the UFO theory. He had obviously been somewhere during those five days – but no one had reported seeing him, and the way his body reappeared was very odd. It was found in broad daylight on top of a coal pile without easy access, and in the vicinity of a busy railway line. No one had reported seeing anything odd during those hours; any effort to place the body in that particular location would have been a hard and cumbersome task, almost certainly resulting in footmarks or some form of indentations in the coal and immediate vicinity. And it would have been a foolhardy and pointless objective for anyone wanting to dispose of a body in the first place. The idea that he had simply dropped from the sky seemed as likely a theory as any.

We should also consider, however, where and when he went missing. Had Zigmund Adamski disappeared during the hours of darkness it would be quite understandable – many hundreds of people go missing at night – but it was early Friday afternoon in late spring when Adamski set off on his errand, and so it seems even more astonishing that no one saw him after that point. The fact that he never reached the shop obviously means that something happened to him on the way there. But what? Even if the UFO abduction theory was considered as a serious alternative, it would still sound implausible in light of this factor alone. What did they do? Beam him up in broad daylight – like Scotty does in *Star Trek?*

Zigmund Adamski has been described as a loving family man, with no known enemies. Although dogged by bad health, he had a lot to live for. Here was a man who had been a prisoner of war, escaped the horror of the Nazis, settled and married and worked in England, only to die in the most mysterious of circumstances.

I have included the mystery here with all the best intentions. Certainly not to cause more grief to the family of the deceased, but in the hope that one day an answer will be forthcoming. Perhaps a reader of this volume will take up the challenge and throw new light on what has been dubbed Yorkshire's mystery of the century?

The Haunting of Heath Farm

Heath Farm is situated on the edge of the busy Dewsbury to Wakefield road – a more unlikely setting for a modern-day haunting would be difficult to imagine.

Built over a network of old mining tunnels, part of the farm is thought to date back to the 17th century. Once owned by the National Coal Board, until they forfeited ownership by losing the deeds to the land, it was sold to Mr Roger Sales.

Jackie and Graham Johnson took up residence in 1991, only after waiting two years for the price to drop in auction. However, when they moved in to Heath Farm they found that they had inherited something which was not mentioned in the sales brochure. Their attempts to find out more about the history of the property were largely unsuccessful.

Legend has it that the heath on which the farm stands has always had the reputation of being haunted. A single brick-lined tunnel leads from Heath Farm to the pub across the road which is thought to have been built on the site of the local gallows. The rugby club, three-quarters of a mile away, stands in a direct line with the farm and the pub, and was exorcised in the early 1990s, after players and staff were troubled by the ghost of a young boy. Some local people have had eerie experiences there too. Children used to rush into the farm's properties as a 'dare', and a postman told of how he once saw a young boy in ancient dress, and surrounded by a strange glow, sitting at the side of the road crying.

The reasons behind Mr Sales' sudden departure have never been fully explained, but when the couple first visited the farm they found various odd things. The light bulbs in one room suddenly exploded for no accountable reason, and they found salt sprinkled on the window sills, and in the corners, of the farmhouse, a devil's head doorknocker and a pentagram painted on the barn wall!

Also, there is a 'water problem' at Heath Farm. Animals can never be kept on the land, as the stables have constantly had to be rebuilt because of flooding. There seems to be a strange connection to water inside the farmhouse, too. One day, while Graham was running the bath, he went downstairs to chat to Jackie – and only a couple of minutes later water began to drop from the kitchen ceiling above them, which stands directly below the bathroom. Graham wondered how the bath could have filled up so quickly and overflowed, but he bounded up the stairs only to find the bath just half-full, with not the slightest sign of dampness. On inspection, the bath and pipes were totally undamaged, and the kitchen ceiling dried very quickly leaving no water mark.

Jackie considers herself to be a natural psychic, but has never gone on to develop that talent because most of the messages she receives seem to be bad. However, through her 'gift', she has become convinced that there are many spirits evident at Heath Farm. Jackie has seen a stocky lady with dark hair who appears in the farmyard, feeding chickens from her apron. She is thought to be responsible for switching the oven off when guests are expected for dinner!

Another spirit is that of an elderly man who sits in the corner of the workshop and disappears after a while. Workers from a local double glazing company downed tools and refused to work in the room when the old man kept appearing to watch them. The man is thought to be responsible for switching various machines and lights on and off and opening the workshop door at 3.30 pm every day without fail. However, Jackie and Graham say that they quickly got used to it, and are now no longer unnerved by his frequent appearances, disappearances and pranks.

The building which houses the farm offices seemed to be haunted by an unseen entity who sends electrical machines haywire, including phones and faxes. Interestingly, this sound likes poltergeist activity, focused on a particular person. When Jackie is particularly stressed or wound-up she always takes a wide detour around the fax machine, because it starts printing out paper on its own.

The Johnsons had a visit from journalist Christine Wood, who was writing an article for the magazine of strange phenomena, *Fortean Times*, and she was shown around the farm's office building. At the time, Graham was frantically searching for a bunch of keys which he seemed to have mislaid. Christine had been idly staring at the front of the paper-shredding machine and, without moving away from the area, became aware that the keys were suddenly there. She was a little sceptical of it being caused by paranormal phenomena and wondered if it was a crude parlour trick, though pointing out that no one had been near the front of the machine in that time. Also, there was no evidence of trickery, no string or wire nearby and it was such a large cumbersome bunch of keys that the idea that someone had been playing a trick on her seemed very unlikely and virtually impossible. When Christine pointed out to Graham where the keys were, he made no attempt to suggest their reappearance had anything to do with the haunting. She had already been told that the main trick played in the office is hiding pens and keys, so Christine thought that perhaps the entity was simply trying to prove a point. Quite a mystery, thought Christine.

The main entity resident at Heath Farm appears to Jackie as much more sinister, and one which has a stronger influence. Often referred to as the Black Entity by her friend, professional medium Jeanette Ryan, it appears not to be the spirit of a human at all. Jackie calls it Beelzebub (pronounced Bee-elzi-bub). It is around 3'6" tall, is as hairy as a bear and has no human features, with a hunched back and 'piggy' legs. Jackie always knows when Beelzebub is around because there is a dirty, sweaty smell and when it touches her she gets an electric shock.

Her first sighting of this curious entity was while lying in bed one evening when Graham was away on business. Curiously, it appeared as a sort of dark shadow and could only be seen in any detail through the reflection in their wardrobe mirror.

It hung from the ceiling with an odd 'I know something you don't' expression on its face. Jackie was terrified and hid her head under the bedsheet, praying for it to go away, and it did after about 15 minutes.

Christine Wood asked if this could have been nothing more than a bizarre and vivid nightmare. Apparently not, as the entity has also been witnessed by Graham. This time they both saw it again through the mirrored wardrobe, and it seemed to be jumping up and down outside their bedroom window, in a rather agitated fashion. When the couple reached the window and peered out they found it was being upset by one of their cats which they keep locked up in the stables at night.

The third sighting occurred one Christmas, when the couple had placed a novelty Christmas wreath on the front door which played a familiar tune whenever anyone approached the house. One evening, Jackie heard the music and was confused when she peered out of the window to find no one near the house, and no cars in the drive. When the tune constantly replayed, she decided to go outside and investigate and saw Beelzebub darting back and forth in front of the sensor making the music play over and over again! By this time, Jackie wasn't frightened – just angry – and chased the entity across the farmyard, where it disappeared. She admits to feeling quite sorry for it, after that little episode.

Other odd happenings at Heath Farm are curious, to say the least, and remain a complete mystery. What Jack and Graham term 'cloning' could possibly be better described as the appearance of 'ghosts of the living' or 'doppelgangers'.

Jackie once saw Graham appear in the kitchen then proceed to walk upstairs. After she called upstairs to tell him that dinner was ready, she found him in one of the offices at the other end of the building. There was only one staircase leading up to the upper floor, and the foot of the stairs had never been out of her sight for more than a few seconds.

One evening, Craig, an office worker at Heath Farm, called one of their dogs, Sassy. He watched her bounding across the field 500 yards away, and wondered if she could hear him. He was about to call again, but something made him look down to his side. Sassy was sitting there quite patiently. This happened on several occasions.

Phantom echoes are another phenomenon experienced by the workers. Oft-repeated phrases like 'call the dog' or 'call the horse' are often heard being thrown back across the yard after the person has just uttered them. Again, not particularly scary – just extremely puzzling.

On one occasion, the couple's manager Roger promised to tape a programme for them about a clergyman performing an exorcism in nearby Hull. On the couple's return from their night out, they ran the tape and heard a 'horrible voice' over the commentary which was talking about evil and the devil. As the actual exorcism ceremony on the programme was about to start, the tape switched itself off.

They asked Roger to take it home with him and test it on his own video recorder, which he did, and it worked perfectly.

Even in the early days, before they moved to the farm, Jeanette Ryan strongly advised the couple not to buy the property. Even now, she says that the best advice she can give them is to 'get the hell out of there'.

Jeanette visited the farm with Ken Mann, from the local newspaper, *The Dewsbury Reporter*, in early summer 1998, and had a strange experience while Ken was photographing her. On one of the photographs, Jeanette is holding a talisman designed to ward off evil spirits. However, both photos were partly blacked out by odd shapes. Mr Mann said that in his 25 years as a photographer he had never seen anything like it. He knew there was nothing to account for it as he peered through the viewfinder as the pictures were taken – no camera case, no fingers, nothing. He said he didn't believe in ghosts or anything of that nature – but could not find an explanation for the shapes on the photographs.

Jeanette has seen some of the spirits which Jackie has glimpsed – and a few more besides. There is a woman who cries for her child in the kitchen; a man called Ted who carries a shotgun protecting the farm; a group of children, all of them plague victims, who may be responsible for the strange goings-on in the office building; a man who hanged himself on the property; and the Black Entity, or Beelzebub, who is by far the strongest of them all.

Jackie believes that a lot of bad luck has befallen the couple because of the farm's phantom influences. Some of their pet dogs have died in mysterious circumstances, Graham's health has deteriorated while living there, and a number of business contracts have been lost to lower bids from companies which have since folded, though it would be unwise to say whether or not this has a direct bearing on the ghostly happenings!

Having said that, Jackie believes that the various entities don't mean them any real harm. However, the atmosphere in the house never lifts, and the only time Jackie and Graham feel better is when they leave the premises. What 'it' can do and what it creates does frighten her, and she added that they are both deeply unhappy, but have no choice for the moment but to live with it.

Secondhand Spook

June and Peter Henderson have lived in the same terraced house in Doncaster for over ten years, since they moved from Royton, in Lancashire. The bought the property from the relatives of an elderly gentleman who lived there until his death in June 1990, and agree that the house itself has always had a very relaxed and welcoming atmosphere.

Five years passed at their address with nothing untoward happening – paranormal or otherwise – until one fateful day in March 1995. The couple went for a day out in Keighley and read somewhere that there was

A cupboard with a story

due to be an auction at a house clearance organised by a local estate agent. Always keen to spot a bargain, they arrived at the old house just outside the town centre and viewed the wares on offer. The one item which caught June's attention was an old cupboard measuring six feet high by three feet wide. She mentioned to her husband that it would provide much-needed storage space in the spare bedroom, which was now empty since their sons had moved away. When the auction started, there was little competition for the cupboard, and the couple secured it at a bargain price.

The estate agents kindly offered free delivery and the driver and his mate even carried it up their stairs for them when it arrived two days later. The Hendersons spent the next hour filling it up with some of the clutter from their own bedroom, and their task was soon completed. June mentioned that she had been unable to find one of her old dresses which she was sure she had kept and went to their bedroom to find it, while Peter stayed in the spare room.

Peter Henderson will remember that day for the rest of his life.

Suddenly, the temperature dropped to freezing level. It was so sudden and without warning it made him gasp. It was not a warm day – but not particularly cold either. The windows were closed, and while there was always a slight draught from them, he could not attribute this sensation to that. The next thing he heard was the toilet flushing. Funny, he thought. He hadn't seen June go to the bathroom. She had gone to their bedroom on the right of the spare room, and he had not seen her walk past the door to reach the bathroom. He walked out of the room, onto the landing and pushed open the bathroom door. The toilet had indeed flushed, the bowl was filling up with water again, but June was not there.

Understandable then, that when June appeared behind him and touched his arm, he jumped a little. Peter asked if she had been to the bathroom, but she hadn't. Of course she hadn't. She couldn't have reached the bathroom, or left it, without him seeing her. Strange, too, that she hadn't heard the toilet flush either, although they could both hear the water pipes filling up again. He decided not to mention the cold spot by the cupboard, but just shook his head, mentioned that there must be something wrong with the plumbing, and simply left it at that.

About an hour later, as they were watching TV in the living room, they both heard a single bump from upstairs. It wasn't a loud bang as if something had exploded, just a slight, but distinct thud which startled them a little, and they exchanged glances. Without saying a word, Peter got to his feet and went upstairs to take a look, with June close behind. What they saw astounded them. A small stool from the spare bedroom was lying on the floor of their own bedroom!

The couple just stood and looked on open-mouthed. They agreed that neither of them had taken the stool from the spare room and put it there. There was no reason they would have needed to do that anyway. The stool was always kept by the other side of the spare bed, between the bed and the window. June rarely moved it except for cleaning and she hadn't cleaned the room for quite a while. And even if they had moved it, how had it fallen over? It was a complete mystery. They returned the stool to its original position in the spare room, and went back downstairs.

For a week, nothing else happened. Neither of them went into the spare room as they had no reason to do so. The odd chill which they both noticed from time to time, always around the door of the room, and at the top of the stairs on the landing, did not strike them as strange enough to merit discussion. In fact, they only found out about their mutual experiences of the chill, when they experienced it together one day. It was exactly a week since they had bought the cupboard, when they revisited the room. June was the first in and what she saw stopped her dead in her tracks. She called to Peter and he rushed up the stairs to see what was wrong.

All of the clothes and shoes and other belongings which they had put carefully into the cupboard were strewn all over the bed. Their eyes went directly to where the stool should have been – but it wasn't and they found it wedged behind the door. The doors of the cupboard itself were closed – so even if by some ludicrous stretch of the imagination, a heavy traffic vibration or freak earth tremor had knocked all the belongings out of the cupboard, the doors would not have shut themselves. It was then that June and Peter told each other of the sudden icy chills they had both experienced over the last week. They decided not to move anything, leaving the clothes and stool where they found them, and hurriedly left the room, closing the door behind them. However, as they made their way back downstairs, a sudden chill hit Peter, which he later said felt as if someone had shot right through him. June experienced the same thing and the 'sensation' whooshed right past them as if it had sprinted upstairs.

Neither Peter or June had ever been very religious or spiritual or had the slightest of interest or belief in the paranormal, but they could not find any other explanation for what they had experienced. Although the last thing they wanted to do was go telling everyone about it, they knew they needed help. A flick through the Yellow Pages revealed a short list of spiritualist churches in the area and, even though the couple were apprehensive about contacting them, they decided to give it a try.

Following a telephone call to one of the numbers, they welcomed a